Spring-clean those Maths skills with CGP!

Blow away the winter cobwebs with this CGP Daily Practice Book — it'll help pupils' Maths skills sparkle in the spring sunshine!

There's a page of brilliant Maths practice for every school day of the spring term, all covering vital skills from the Year 4 curriculum.

It's perfect for use in class or at home, with plenty of examples and splashes of colour to keep things interesting. Bring on spring!

What CGP is all about

Our sole aim here at CGP is to produce the highest quality books — carefully written, immaculately presented and dangerously close to being funny.

Then we work our socks off to get them out to you — at the cheapest possible prices.

Contents

☑ Use the tick boxes to help keep a record of which tests have been attempted.

Week 1
- ☑ Day 1 1
- ☑ Day 2 2
- ☑ Day 3 3
- ☑ Day 4 4
- ☑ Day 5 5

Week 2
- ☑ Day 1 6
- ☑ Day 2 7
- ☑ Day 3 8
- ☑ Day 4 9
- ☑ Day 5 10

Week 3
- ☑ Day 1 11
- ☑ Day 2 12
- ☑ Day 3 13
- ☑ Day 4 14
- ☑ Day 5 15

Week 4
- ☑ Day 1 16
- ☑ Day 2 17
- ☑ Day 3 18
- ☑ Day 4 19
- ☑ Day 5 20

Week 5
- ☑ Day 1 21
- ☑ Day 2 22
- ☑ Day 3 23
- ☑ Day 4 24
- ☑ Day 5 25

Week 6
- ☑ Day 1 26
- ☑ Day 2 27
- ☑ Day 3 28
- ☑ Day 4 29
- ☑ Day 5 30

Week 7
- ☑ Day 1 31
- ☑ Day 2 32
- ☑ Day 3 33
- ☑ Day 4 34
- ☑ Day 5 35

Week 8
- ☑ Day 1 36
- ☑ Day 2 37
- ☑ Day 3 38
- ☑ Day 4 39
- ☑ Day 5 40

Week 9
- [✓] Day 1 41
- [✓] Day 2 42
- [✓] Day 3 43
- [✓] Day 4 44
- [✓] Day 5 45

Week 10
- [✓] Day 1 46
- [✓] Day 2 47
- [✓] Day 3 48
- [✓] Day 4 49
- [✓] Day 5 50

Week 11
- [✓] Day 1 51
- [✓] Day 2 52
- [✓] Day 3 53
- [✓] Day 4 54
- [✓] Day 5 55

Week 12
- [✓] Day 1 56
- [✓] Day 2 57
- [✓] Day 3 58
- [✓] Day 4 59
- [✓] Day 5 60

Answers 61

Published by CGP

ISBN: 978 1 78908 653 9

Editors: Katie Fernandez, Sarah Pattison, Rachael Rogers, George Wright

With thanks to Paul Jordin and Emma Wright for the proofreading.

With thanks to Lottie Edwards for the copyright research.

Clipart from Corel®

Printed by W&G Baird Ltd, Antrim.
Based on the classic CGP style created by Richard Parsons.

Text, design, layout and original illustrations © Coordination Group Publications Ltd. (CGP) 2020
All rights reserved.

Photocopying this book is not permitted, even if you have a CLA licence.
Extra copies are available from CGP with next day delivery • 0800 1712 712 • www.cgpbooks.co.uk

How to Use this Book

- This book contains 60 daily practice tests.
- We've split them into 12 sections — that's roughly one for each week of the Year 4 spring term.
- Each week is made up of 5 tests, so there's one for every school day of the term (Monday – Friday).
- Each test should take about 10 minutes to complete.
- The tests contain a mix of topics from Year 4 Maths. New Year 4 topics are gradually introduced as you go through the book.
- The tests increase in difficulty as you progress through the term.
- Each test looks something like this:

The Week and the Day of the test are shown at the top of the page.

The instruction the pupil needs to follow is in the box at the top of the page.

There's an example at the top of the page. The correct answer is shown in red. Talk the pupil through the instruction and the example so they know what to do.

There are between 4 and 12 questions for the pupil to answer.

There's a score box at the bottom of the test. Use this to keep track of how well the pupil has done.

Week 1 — Day 1

Put the decimals in order, starting with the smallest.

	1.41	1.23	0.97	1.03
	0.97	1.03	1.23	1.41
	smallest			largest

1) 1.86   0.64   1.25   1.43

smallest ☐ ☐ ☐ ☐ largest

2) 0.21   1.60   1.18   1.80

smallest ☐ ☐ ☐ ☐ largest

3) 1.79   1.49   0.67   1.06

smallest ☐ ☐ ☐ ☐ largest

4) 1.35   1.26   1.92   1.84

smallest ☐ ☐ ☐ ☐ largest

5) 1.29   1.47   1.08   1.74

smallest ☐ ☐ ☐ ☐ largest

6) 1.38   1.14   1.10   1.89

smallest ☐ ☐ ☐ ☐ largest

7) 1.76   1.72   1.94   1.82

smallest ☐ ☐ ☐ ☐ largest

8) 1.32   1.56   1.45   1.54

smallest ☐ ☐ ☐ ☐ largest

Today I scored ☐ out of 8.

Week 1 — Day 2

Fill in the boxes to complete the steps of 1000.

Example: −1000 ← 2211 → +1000, giving 1211 and 3211.

1) −1000 ← 6644 → +1000

2) −1000 ← 7368 → +1000

3) −1000 → 5422 → +1000 (middle box empty, 5422 is the −1000 result)

4) −1000 → [ ] → +1000 → 4536

5) −1000 ← 2179 → +1000

6) −1000 → [ ] → +1000 → 9887

7) −1000 → [ ] → +1000 → 3953

8) −1000 ← 8795 → +1000

9) −1000 → 1342 → +1000 (1342 is the −1000 result)

10) −1000 → [ ] → +1000 → 7925

11) −1000 → 4688 → +1000 (4688 is the −1000 result)

12) −1000 → [ ] → +1000 → 5876

Today I scored ☐ out of 12.

Week 1 — Day 3

Look at the number and answer the question.

952.34
Which digit is in the tenths place? 3

1) 375.21
Which digit is in the tenths place?

2) 681.97
Which digit is in the hundredths place?

3) 236.73
Which digit is in the ones place?

4) 428.16
Which digit is in the hundredths place?

5) 147.89
Which digit is in the tenths place?

6) 513.48
Which digit is in the hundreds place?

7) 769.52
Which digit is in the tenths place?

8) 894.65
Which digit is in the tens place?

9) 316.42
Which digit is in the tenths place?

10) 742.81
Which digit is in the hundredths place?

11) 537.94
Which digit is in the tenths place?

12) 985.36
Which digit is in the hundredths place?

Today I scored ☐ out of 12.

Week 1 — Day 4

Fill in the missing number in the calculation.

$92 \div \boxed{10} = 9.2$

1) $7 \div \boxed{} = 0.7$

2) $5 \div 10 = \boxed{}$

3) $31 \div \boxed{} = 3.1$

4) $4 \div \boxed{} = 0.4$

5) $3 \div \boxed{} = 0.03$

6) $16 \div \boxed{} = 0.16$

7) $43 \div 100 = \boxed{}$

8) $86 \div 10 = \boxed{}$

9) $10 \div \boxed{} = 0.1$

10) $90 \div 100 = \boxed{}$

11) $22 \div \boxed{} = 2.2$

12) $6 \div 100 = \boxed{}$

Today I scored ☐ out of 12.

Week 1 — Day 5

Circle the name of the person who has more money.

Eliana has twenty £1 coins.
Arlo has five £2 coins and nine 50p coins.

1. Merlin has ten 20p coins.
   Annika has sixteen 10p coins and ten 5p coins.

   Merlin   Annika

2. Elsie has twelve 50p coins.
   Forrest has three £1 coins and two £2 coins.

   Elsie   Forrest

3. Iwan has ten 50p coins.
   Dahlia has three £1 coins and five 20p coins.

   Iwan   Dahlia

4. Tyra has four £2 coins.
   Ciaran has four £1 coins and six 50p coins.

   Tyra   Ciaran

5. Tahir has forty £1 coins.
   Lacey has eighteen £2 coins and seven 50p coins.

   Tahir   Lacey

6. Nina has one hundred 20p coins.
   Mack has eight £2 coins and ten 50p coins.

   Nina   Mack

7. Aidan has fifteen £2 coins.
   Faiza has twenty six £1 coins and ten 20p coins.

   Aidan   Faiza

8. Em has one hundred 50p coins.
   Moa has twenty two £2 coins and twelve 20p coins.

   Em   Moa

Today I scored ☐ out of 8.

Week 2 — Day 1

Write the fraction as a decimal. $\frac{1}{10}$ = 0.1

1) $\frac{3}{10}$ =

2) $\frac{9}{10}$ =

3) $\frac{64}{100}$ =

4) $\frac{17}{100}$ =

5) $\frac{7}{10}$ =

6) $\frac{32}{100}$ =

7) $\frac{1}{2}$ =

8) $\frac{99}{100}$ =

9) $\frac{3}{4}$ =

10) $\frac{5}{100}$ =

11) $\frac{50}{100}$ =

12) $\frac{2}{100}$ =

Today I scored ☐ out of 12.

Week 2 — Day 2

What is the perimeter of the shape? (The shape is not drawn to scale.)

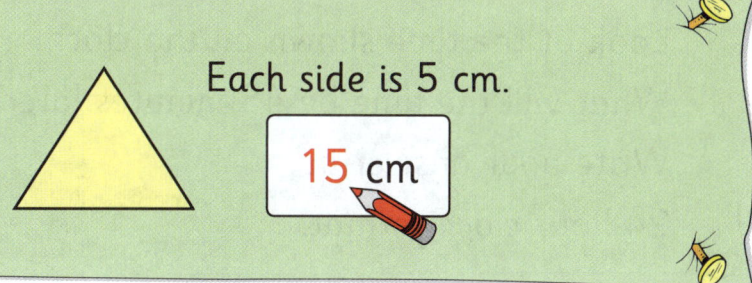

Each side is 5 cm.

15 cm

1. Each side is 8 cm. ___ cm

2. Two sides are 2 cm and two sides are 4 cm. ___ cm

3. Each side is 9 cm. ___ cm

4. Each side is 6 cm. ___ cm

5. Two sides are 6 cm and one side is 4 cm. ___ cm

6. Two sides are 9 cm and two sides are 15 cm. ___ cm

7. Each side is 7 cm. ___ cm

8. Each side is 80 cm. ___ cm

9. Each side is 30 cm. ___ cm

10. Each side is 23 cm. ___ cm

Today I scored ___ out of 10.

Week 2 — Day 3

Look at the time shown on the clock. What will the time be 45 minutes later? Write your answer in 24-hour clock format.

6:20 pm + 45 minutes → 19:05

1. 11:10 am + 45 minutes →
2. 1:00 am + 45 minutes →
3. 7:01 pm + 45 minutes →
4. 2:15 am + 45 minutes →
5. 3:45 pm + 45 minutes →
6. 4:30 pm + 45 minutes →
7. 6:09 pm + 45 minutes →
8. 9:45 pm + 45 minutes →
9. 10:20 pm + 45 minutes →
10. 7:52 am + 45 minutes →
11. 8:33 pm + 45 minutes →
12. 11:59 pm + 45 minutes →

Today I scored ☐ out of 12.

Year 4 Maths — Spring Term

Week 2 — Day 4

What number is the arrow pointing to?

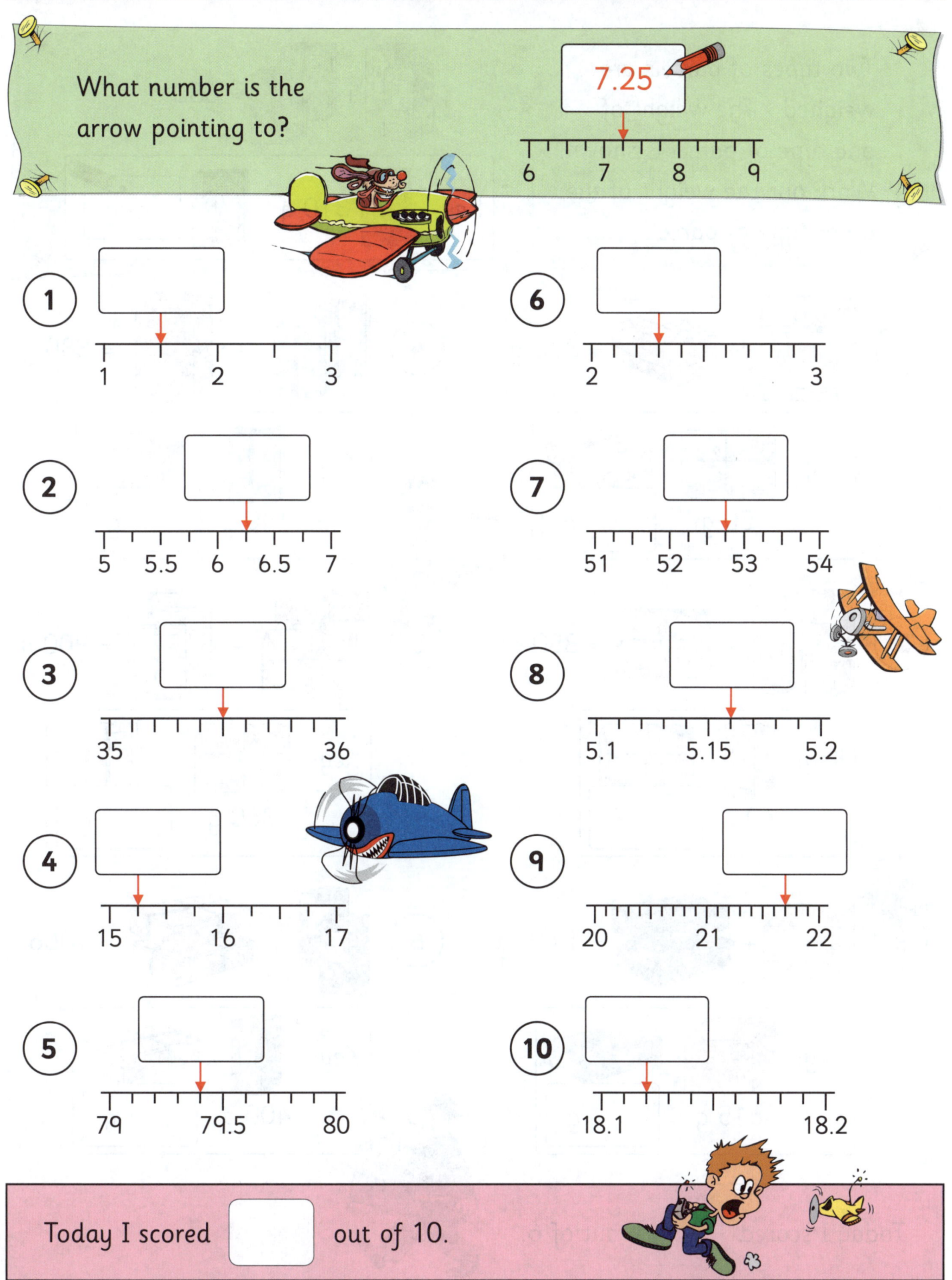

Today I scored ☐ out of 10.

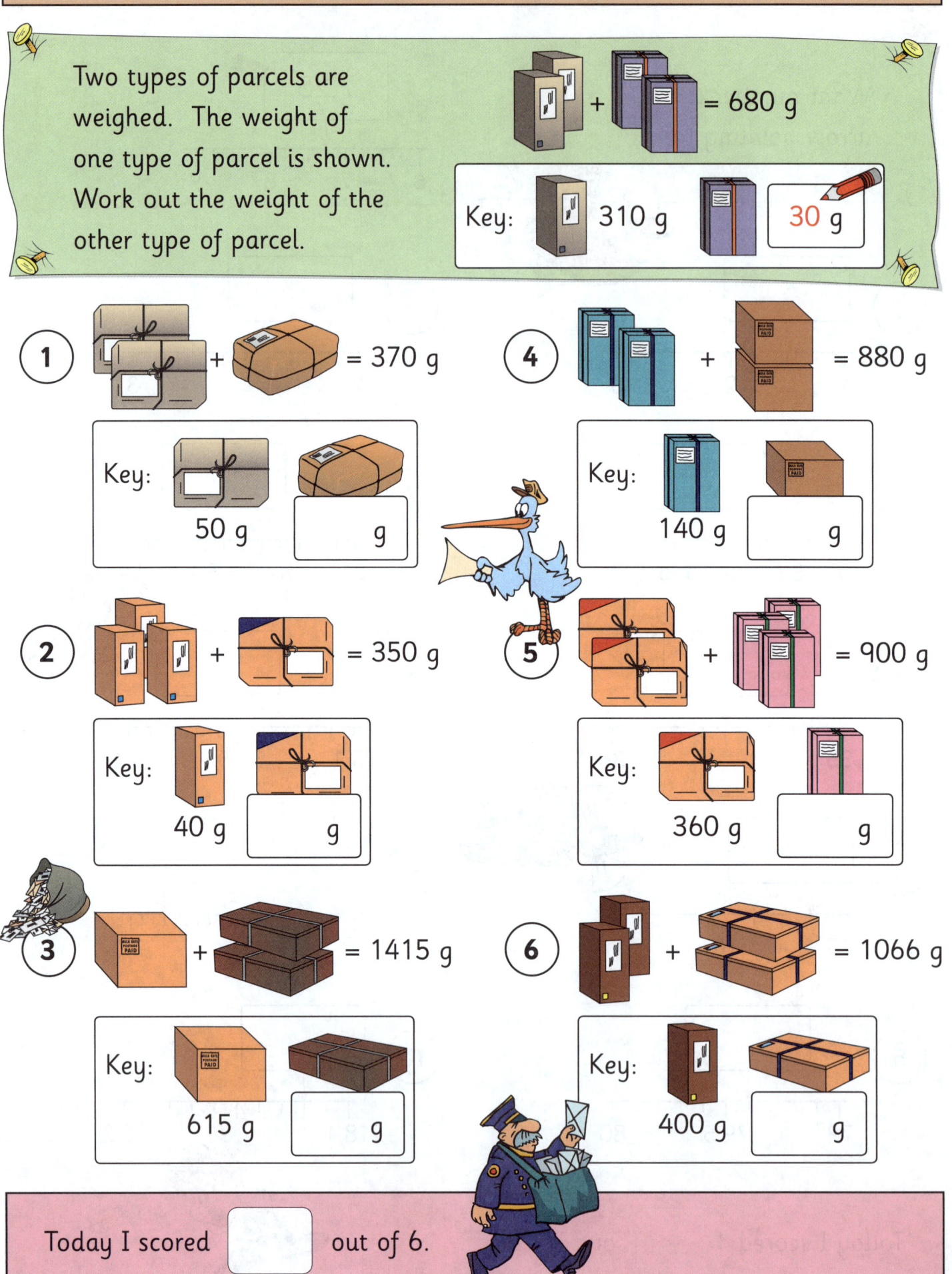

Week 3 — Day 1

Fill in the box to show how many right angles the shape has been rotated in the direction given.

3 right angles clockwise

1.  _____ anticlockwise

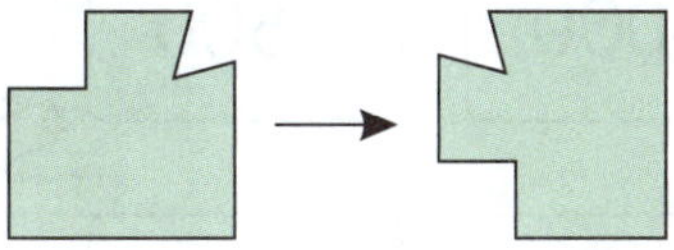

2. _____ clockwise

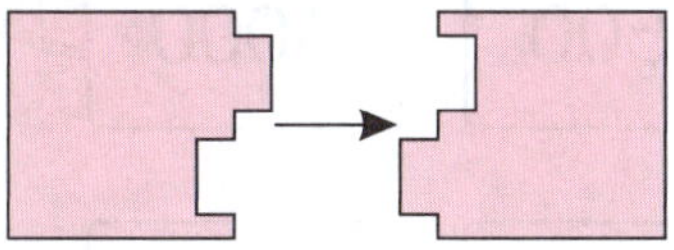

3. _____ anticlockwise

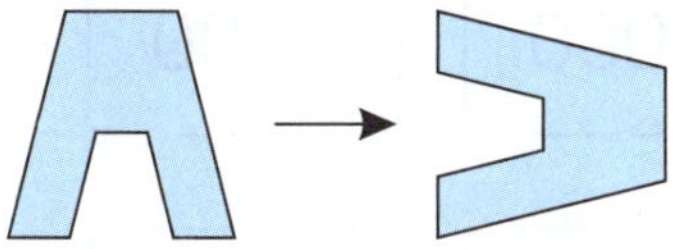

4. _____ clockwise

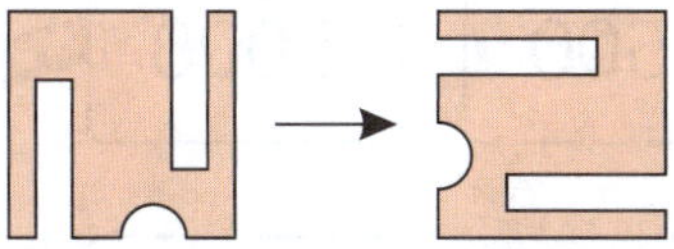

5. _____ anticlockwise

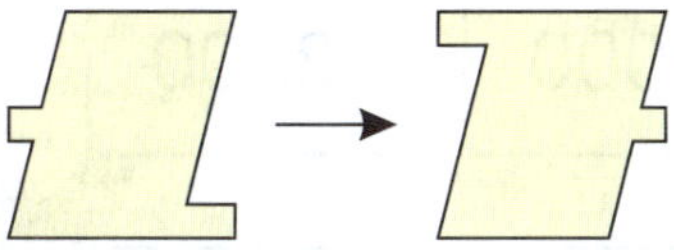

6. _____ clockwise

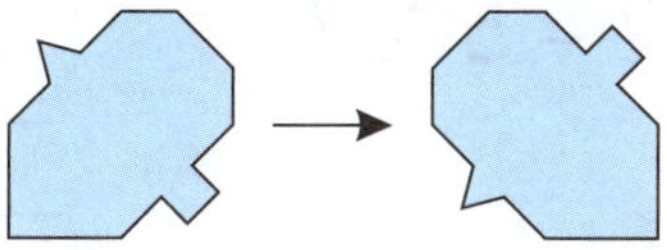

7. _____ clockwise

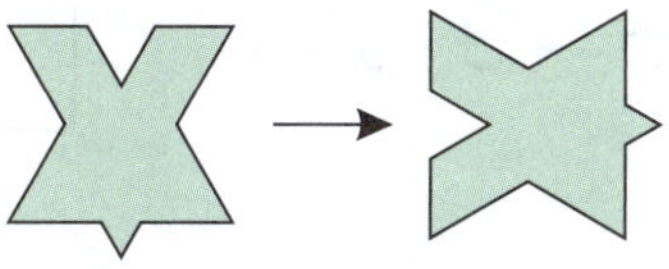

8. 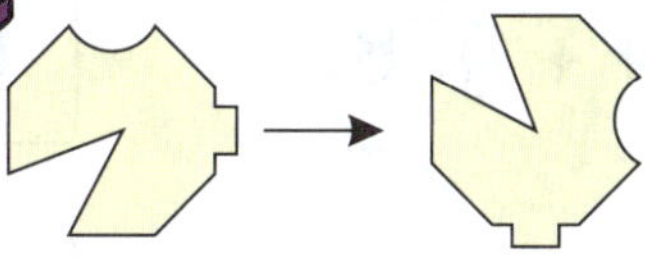 _____ anticlockwise

9. _____ clockwise

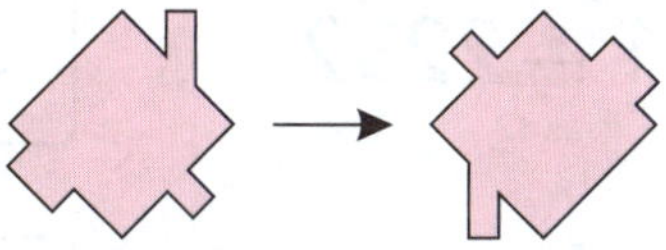

10. _____ anticlockwise

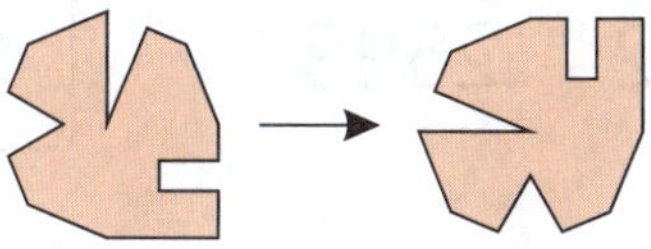

Today I scored _____ out of 10.

Week 3 — Day 2

Circle the best estimate for the answer to the calculation.

7524 − 3966

3000 | (3500) | 4000 | 4500

1) 8972 − 5007 — 3000 | 3500 | 4000 | 4500

2) 4990 + 3534 — 7000 | 7500 | 8000 | 8500

3) 6125 − 3106 — 2500 | 3000 | 3500 | 4000

4) 7107 + 1936 — 8000 | 8500 | 9000 | 9500

5) 2904 + 4587 — 6000 | 6500 | 7000 | 7500

6) 9098 − 1582 — 7500 | 8000 | 8500 | 9000

7) 5711 − 2232 — 3500 | 4000 | 4500 | 5000

8) 4173 + 1324 — 5000 | 5500 | 6000 | 6500

9) 6132 − 2598 — 2000 | 2500 | 3000 | 3500

10) 8874 − 5421 — 3000 | 3500 | 4000 | 4500

Today I scored ☐ out of 10.

Year 4 Maths — Spring Term

Week 3 — Day 3

Work out how long the sports practice lasted.

Charis' fencing practice usually lasts for 1 hour. This week it was 11 minutes shorter.

49 minutes

1. Emily's dance practice usually lasts for 1 hour. This week it was 8 minutes longer. — minutes

2. Lauren's football practice usually lasts for 1 hour. This week it was 9 minutes shorter. — minutes

3. Jordan's basketball practice usually lasts for 1 hour. This week it was 14 minutes shorter. — minutes

4. John's golf practice usually lasts for 1 hour. This week it was 12 minutes longer. — minutes

5. Elspeth's gymnastics practice usually lasts for 1 hour. This week it was 21 minutes longer. — minutes

6. Alexa's netball practice usually lasts for 2 hours. This week it was 20 minutes shorter. — minutes

7. Luke's badminton practice usually lasts for 2 hours. This week it was 6 minutes longer. — minutes

8. Liz's hockey practice usually lasts for 2 hours. This week it was 16 minutes shorter. — minutes

9. Arthur's ballet practice usually lasts for 3 hours. This week it was 7 minutes longer. — minutes

10. Lloyd's boccia practice usually lasts for 3 hours. This week it was 13 minutes shorter. — minutes

Today I scored ☐ out of 10.

Week 3 — Day 4

Write the measurement in the units given.

2 m = 200 cm

1) 4 km = ☐ m

2) 5000 ml = ☐ litres

3) 8 m = ☐ cm

4) 3.2 kg = ☐ g

5) 2900 ml = ☐ litres

6) 5.6 m = ☐ cm

7) 0.8 kg = ☐ g

8) 1.5 km = ☐ m

9) 650 ml = ☐ litres

10) 10.7 m = ☐ cm

11) 15.8 kg = ☐ g

12) 0.93 km = ☐ m

Today I scored ☐ out of 12.

Week 3 — Day 5

Calculate how long the journey took.

It takes Brad 20 minutes to run 2 miles.
One day he ran 6 miles.
He stopped to rest for 15 minutes.

1 h **15** min

1. It takes Becca 30 minutes to run 2 miles.
   One day she ran 6 miles.
   She stopped to rest for 10 minutes.

   ☐ h ☐ min

2. It takes Colin 20 minutes to run 3 miles.
   One day he ran 12 miles.
   He stopped to rest for 5 minutes.

   ☐ h ☐ min

3. It takes Ruth 20 minutes to run 2 miles.
   One day she ran 10 miles.
   She stopped to rest for 30 minutes.

   ☐ h ☐ min

4. It takes Azeem 15 minutes to run 2 miles.
   One day he ran 12 miles.
   He stopped to rest for 35 minutes.

   ☐ h ☐ min

5. It takes Aanisa 30 minutes to run 3 miles.
   One day she ran 15 miles.
   She stopped to rest for 20 minutes.

   ☐ h ☐ min

Today I scored ☐ out of 5.

Week 4 — Day 1

Work out the answer to the calculation.

```
  7 6 9 3
+ 2 1 6 5
---------
  9 8 5 8
      1
```

1) 1 0 1 4
   + 4 3 2 1

2) 1 8 3 3
   + 5 4 5 6

3) 4 1 3 2
   + 6 3 6 2

4) 5 0 9 2
   + 4 5 9 0

5) 3 5 1 8
   + 2 6 4 7

6) 4 6 3 9
   + 5 0 7 6

7) 6 4 0 5
   + 2 9 3 6

8) 4 3 0 9
   + 1 9 1 3

9) 3 1 5 6
   + 4 9 6 7

10) 3 1 7 9
   + 5 8 7 2

Today I scored ☐ out of 10.

Year 4 Maths — Spring Term

Week 4 — Day 2

The pictogram shows the favourite lesson chosen by some students.

Work out how many students chose Art or Maths.

Key: ◯ = 8 people

Maths	◐
Art	◯ ◐
P.E.	◯

16

1.

English	◯ ◐
Maths	◯
Art	◯ ◯ ◯

2.

Art	◯ ◯ ◯
Maths	◯ ◯ ◔
Science	◐

3.

Art	◐
Music	◯ ◯
Maths	◯ ◯ ◔

4.

Maths	◯ ◯ ◔
Art	◯ ◯ ◐
P.E.	◕

5.

Geography	◯ ◯ ◕
Maths	◯ ◕
Art	◯ ◐

6.

Art	◯ ◯ ◕
History	◯ ◯ ◐
Maths	◯ ◕

Today I scored ☐ out of 6.

Week 4 — Day 3

Circle the best estimate for the measurement.

The length of a desk.
(1 m) | 10 cm | 1 km

1 The length of a pen.
20 cm | 2 m | 2 cm

2 The weight of a mug.
4 g | 400 g | 4 kg

3 The length of an eraser.
5 m | 50 cm | 5 cm

4 The height of a house's front door.
2 m | 50 cm | 10 m

5 The weight of a pencil.
12 kg | 6 g | 900 g

6 The height of a desk.
5 m | 70 cm | 20 cm

7 The length of a bus.
90 cm | 2 km | 8 m

8 The height of a house.
7 m | 50 m | 6 km

9 The weight of a pineapple.
1 kg | 5 g | 19 kg

10 The weight of a tennis ball.
1 kg | 500 g | 60 g

11 The length of a football pitch.
10 m | 120 m | 2 km

12 The weight of a television.
1 kg | 14 kg | 400 g

Today I scored ☐ out of 12.

Week 4 — Day 4

Lewis needs to buy some ingredients to bake a cake. Tick the option that is cheaper.

- [✓] Three 50 g bags of nuts that cost 70p each.
- [ ] Two 75 g bags of nuts that cost £1.10 each.

1
- [ ] Five 1 kg bags of sugar that cost 70p each.
- [ ] Four 1.25 kg bags of sugar that cost £1 each.

2
- [ ] Four 500 g bags of flour that cost 75p each.
- [ ] Two 1 kg bags of flour that cost £1.25 each.

3
- [ ] Three 80 g bags of chocolate chips that cost £1.50 each.
- [ ] Ten 24 g bags of chocolate chips that cost 50p each.

4
- [ ] Three 400 g packs of butter that cost £1.20 each.
- [ ] Four 300 g packs of butter that cost 80p each.

5
- [ ] Five boxes of 6 eggs that cost 80p each.
- [ ] Two boxes of 15 eggs that cost £1.90 each.

6
- [ ] Five 300 g jars of jam that cost 90p each.
- [ ] Three 500 g jars of jam that cost £1.40 each.

Today I scored ☐ out of 6.

Week 4 — Day 5

48 children picked their favourite colour. The results are shown in the pictogram. Fill in the missing row.

Key: ◇ = 6 children

Red	◇◇◇
Blue	◇◇
Pink	◇◇

1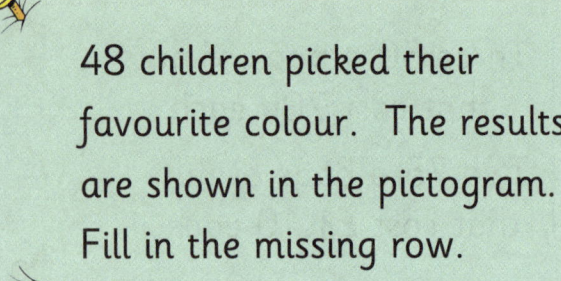

2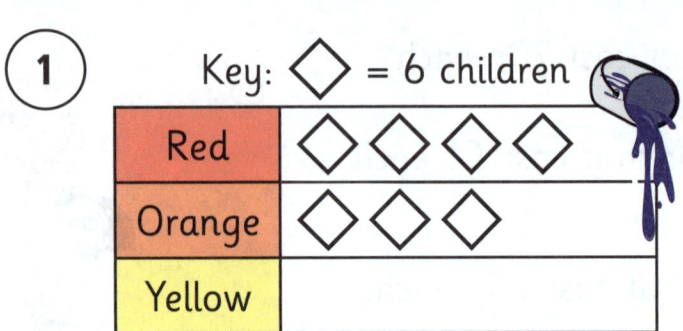

3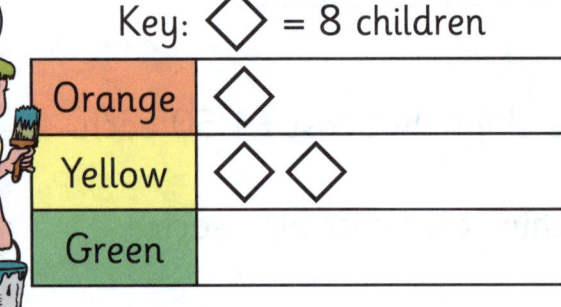

4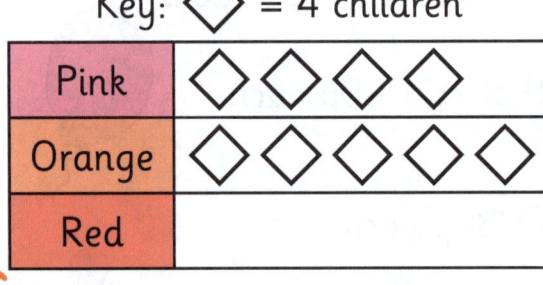

5

6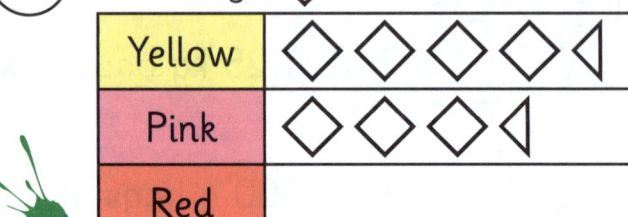

7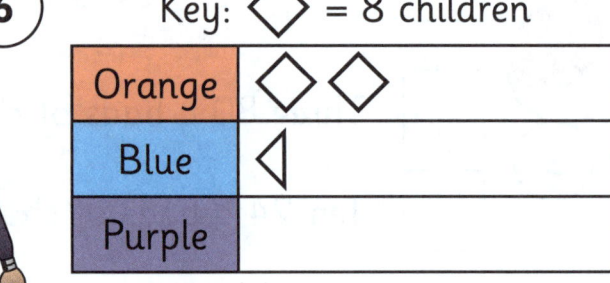

8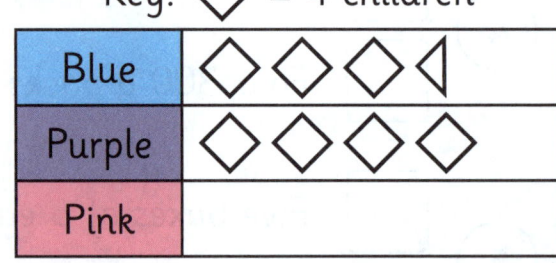

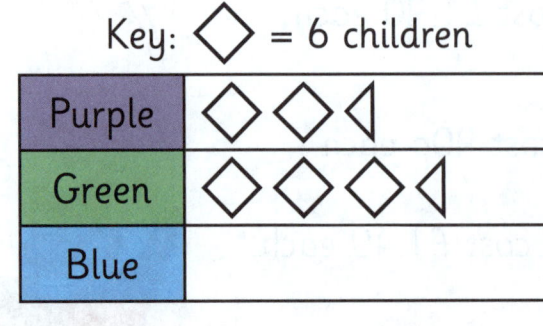
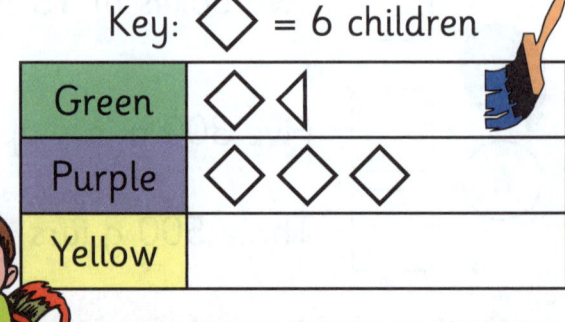

Today I scored ☐ out of 8.

Week 5 — Day 1

Circle the number that is in the seven times table.

34   (28)   20
30   23

1. 7   16   31
    10   18

2. 25   19   12
    24   14

3. 61   68   70
    64   69

4. 38   35   30
    36   32

5. 18   21   25
    20   24

6. 22   27   30
    24   28

7. 78   74   72
    77   73

8. 51   44   41
    45   42

9. 49   46   38
    48   39

10. 72   64   54
    65   63

11. 48   56   62
    55   57

12. 90   81   72
    84   78

Today I scored ☐ out of 12.

Week 5 — Day 2

Solve the calculation.

```
  6 3 7 2
− 2 2 4 1
─────────
  4 1 3 1
```

1)
```
  2 1 7 6
− 1 1 3 0
```

2)
```
  9 3 5 3
− 6 1 0 2
```

3)
```
  6 2 7 7
− 5 0 8 6
```

4)
```
  4 5 6 9
− 1 8 3 4
```

5)
```
  2 6 7 8
− 1 3 8 4
```

6)
```
  3 8 4 9
− 1 0 6 9
```

7)
```
  3 6 5 6
− 2 3 1 7
```

8)
```
  5 0 0 4
− 1 7 0 2
```

9)
```
  9 2 6 6
− 6 6 3 7
```

10)
```
  6 3 1 9
− 2 7 7 1
```

Today I scored ☐ out of 10.

Week 5 — Day 3

Count in steps of 9 to complete the sequence.

9 , 18 , 27 , 36 , 45

1) 36 , 45 , ☐ , ☐ , ☐

2) 72 , 81 , ☐ , ☐ , ☐

3) 63 , 54 , ☐ , ☐ , ☐

4) ☐ , 63 , ☐ , 81 , ☐

5) ☐ , ☐ , 81 , ☐ , 63

6) ☐ , 72 , ☐ , 54 , ☐

7) 117 , ☐ , ☐ , 90 , ☐

8) ☐ , 99 , ☐ , ☐ , 126

Today I scored ☐ out of 8.

Week 5 — Day 4

Draw an arrow to match the clock face to the time that it shows.

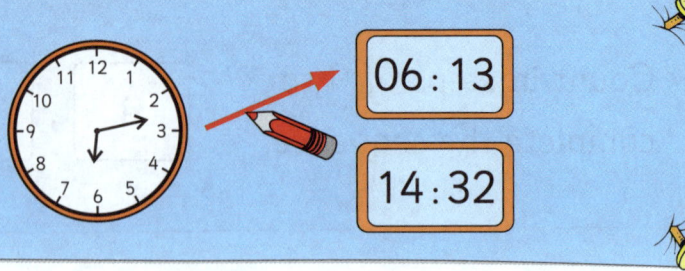

1. 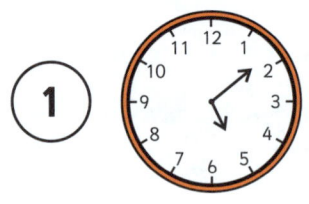 13:26 / 05:08

2. 03:24 / 03:05

3.  20:03 / 12:42

4.  08:16 / 08:32

5. 03:25 / 15:12

6. 08:50 / 09:50

7.  14:20 / 16:20

8. 02:55 / 03:11

9.  16:38 / 17:38

10.  12:05 / 13:06

Today I scored ☐ out of 10.

Week 5 — Day 5

Put the numbers into the calculation to make the largest possible answer. Write the answer in the box.

Numbers: 4, 8, 3

| 8 | 4 | 3 | + 21

Answer = 864

1) Numbers: 0, 9, 0
☐ ☐ ☐ + 84
Answer = ☐

2) Numbers: 9, 0, 5
☐ ☐ ☐ + 37
Answer = ☐

3) Numbers: 1, 9, 0
☐ ☐ ☐ + 49
Answer = ☐

4) Numbers: 1, 8, 3
☐ ☐ ☐ + 15
Answer = ☐

5) Numbers: 2, 9, 4
☐ ☐ ☐ + 36
Answer = ☐

6) Numbers: 2, 2, 6
☐ ☐ ☐ + 59
Answer = ☐

7) Numbers: 2, 6, 7
☐ ☐ ☐ + 29
Answer = ☐

8) Numbers: 5, 2, 7
☐ ☐ ☐ + 85
Answer = ☐

9) Numbers: 7, 8, 2
☐ ☐ ☐ + 52
Answer = ☐

10) Numbers: 5, 7, 4
☐ ☐ ☐ + 97
Answer = ☐

Today I scored ☐ out of 10.

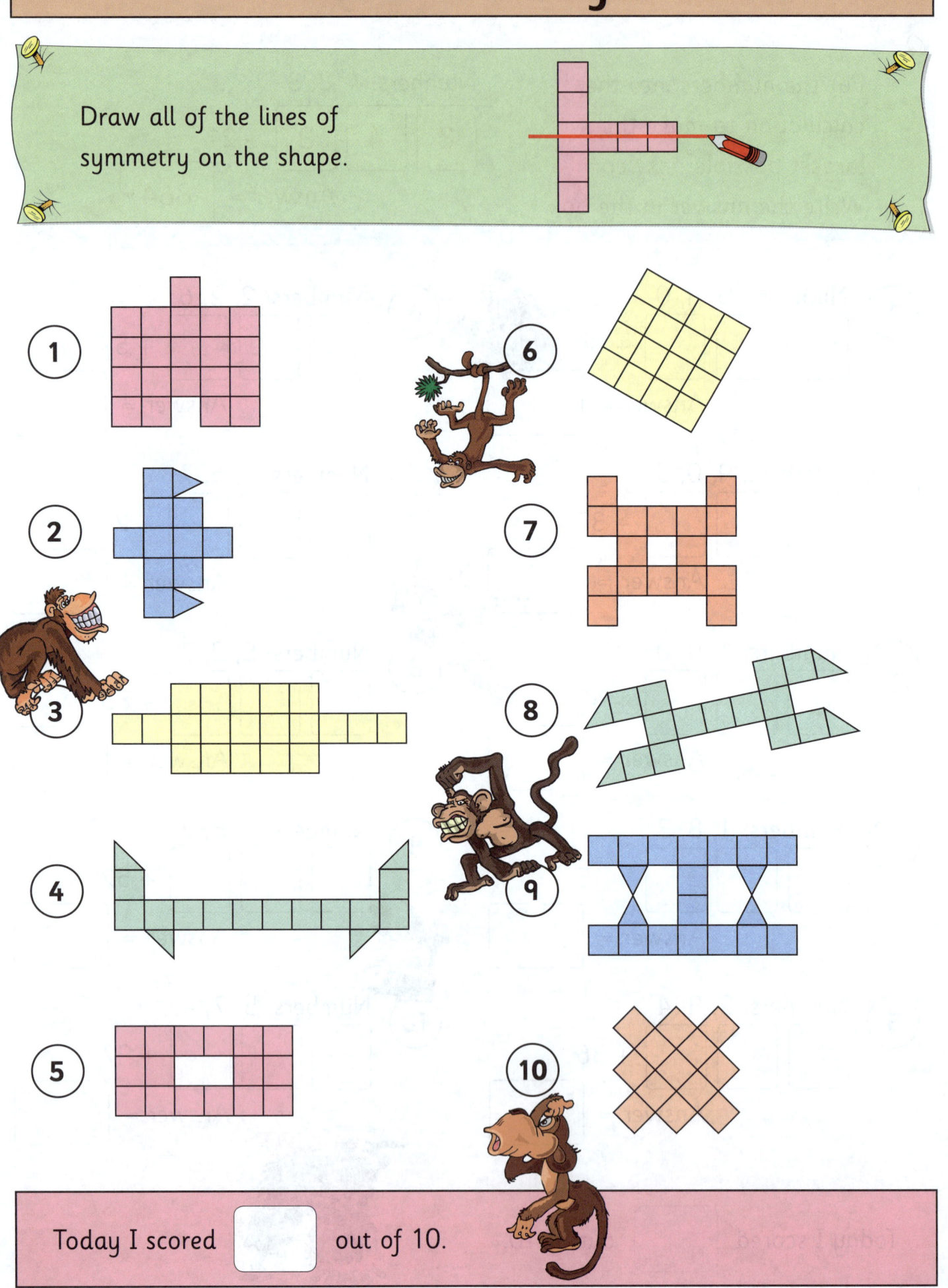

Week 6 — Day 2

Look at the calculation. Write down a calculation you could use to check the answer.

3195 = 1044 + 2151

To check: 3195 − 2151

1. 1150 + 1240 = 2390
   To check:

2. 2700 + 1725 = 4425
   To check:

3. 7900 − 1140 = 6760
   To check:

4. 1255 + 6560 = 7815
   To check:

5. 5099 − 1575 = 3524
   To check:

6. 27.5 + 48.5 = 76
   To check:

7. 41.1 + 50.1 = 91.2
   To check:

8. 6301 = 2489 + 3812
   To check:

9. 6.4 − 1.3 = 5.1
   To check:

10. 1219 = 2544 − 1325
    To check:

11. 7276 = 1569 + 5707
    To check:

12. 2314 = 4368 − 2054
    To check:

Today I scored ☐ out of 12.

Week 6 — Day 3

The bar chart shows the favourite sports of some pupils. Complete the bar chart using the information.

40 pupils chose basketball as their favourite sport. A quarter of this number chose golf.

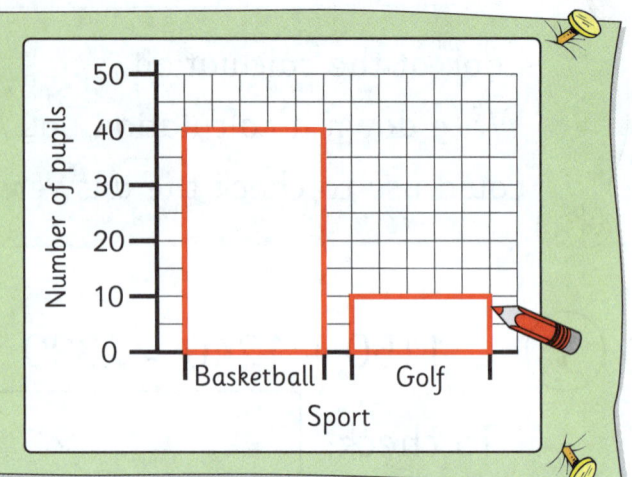

1 4 pupils chose boccia as their favourite sport. 18 pupils chose seatball.

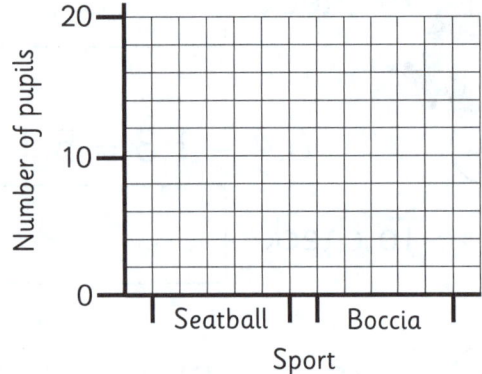

2 25 pupils chose rowing as their favourite sport. This is 15 fewer than the number who chose surfing.

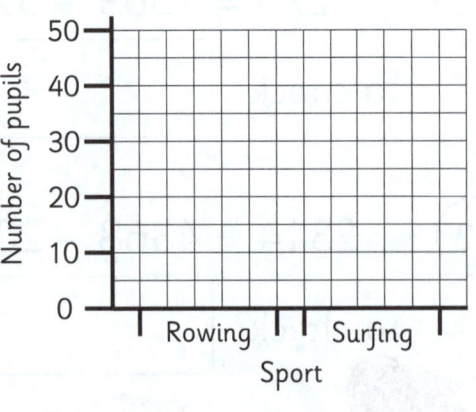

3 90 pupils chose fencing as their favourite sport. This is 3 times the number who chose boxing.

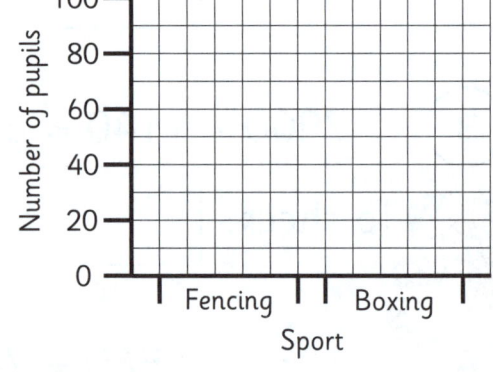

4 60 pupils chose football or dodgeball as their favourite sport. 10 more chose football than dodgeball.

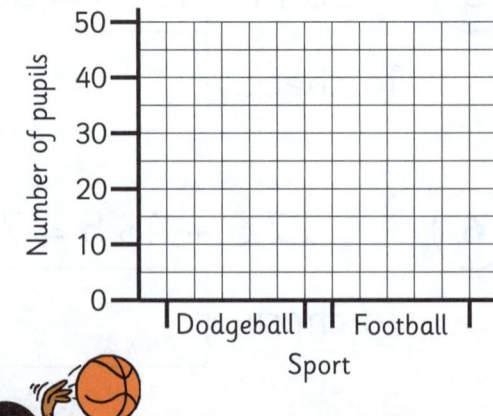

Today I scored ☐ out of 4.

Week 6 — Day 4

How much does the family spend on souvenirs from the zoo?

Meerkat mugs cost £4 each and packs of pencils cost £3 each. The Johnson family buy 12 meerkat mugs and 20 packs of pencils.

£108

1. Banana rubbers cost £1 each and T-shirts cost £5 each. The Beckett family buy 15 banana rubbers and 5 T-shirts.   £

2. Chocolate tigers cost £1 each and mugs cost £4 each. The Smith family buy 11 chocolate tigers and 6 mugs.   £

3. Hippo water bottles cost £10 each and posters cost £4 each. The Gamal family buy 5 hippo water bottles and 8 posters.   £

4. Scarfs cost £5 each and parrot pencils cost £3 each. The Price family buy 9 scarfs and 12 parrot pencils.   £

5. Lion puppets cost £5 each and cuddly lemurs cost £8 each. The Moore family buy 4 lion puppets and 2 cuddly lemurs.   £

6. Giraffe hats cost £8 each and snake straws cost £2 each. The McKenzie family buy 6 giraffe hats and 9 snake straws.   £

7. Baboon pyjama sets cost £9 each and notebooks cost £6 each. The Singh family buy 4 baboon pyjama sets and 3 notebooks.   £

8. Emu pens cost £5 each and elephant masks cost £7 each. The Field family buy 7 emu pens and 8 elephant masks.   £

Today I scored [ ] out of 8.

Week 6 — Day 5

Use the information in the bar chart to answer the question about the fish caught by contestants in a fishing competition.

How many fish did Jo and Jeff catch in total?

22

1) How many fish did the contestants catch in total?

2) How many fish did Mike and Milly catch in total?

3) How many fish did Sam and Sara catch in total?

4) How many fish did Frank, Freya and Fatima catch in total?

Today I scored ☐ out of 4.

Week 7 — Day 1

Work out the answer to each calculation. Add the answers together to work out the total.

5 ÷ 1   12 ÷ 1
11 × 0

Total = 17

1) 7 ÷ 1   1 × 5
   0 × 6
   Total =

2) 30 × 0   1 × 37
   6 × 1
   Total =

3) 17 × 1   14 × 0
   60 ÷ 1
   Total =

4) 1 × 14   71 × 1
   24 × 0
   Total =

5) 13 × 1   30 ÷ 1
   7 ÷ 1
   Total =

6) 0 × 58   14 × 1
   79 ÷ 1
   Total =

7) 1 × 25   36 ÷ 1
   1 × 19
   Total =

8) 93 ÷ 1   0 × 95
   1 × 11
   Total =

9) 14 ÷ 1   99 × 1
   70 ÷ 1
   Total =

10) 1 × 55   18 ÷ 1
    29 × 1
    Total =

Today I scored ☐ out of 10.

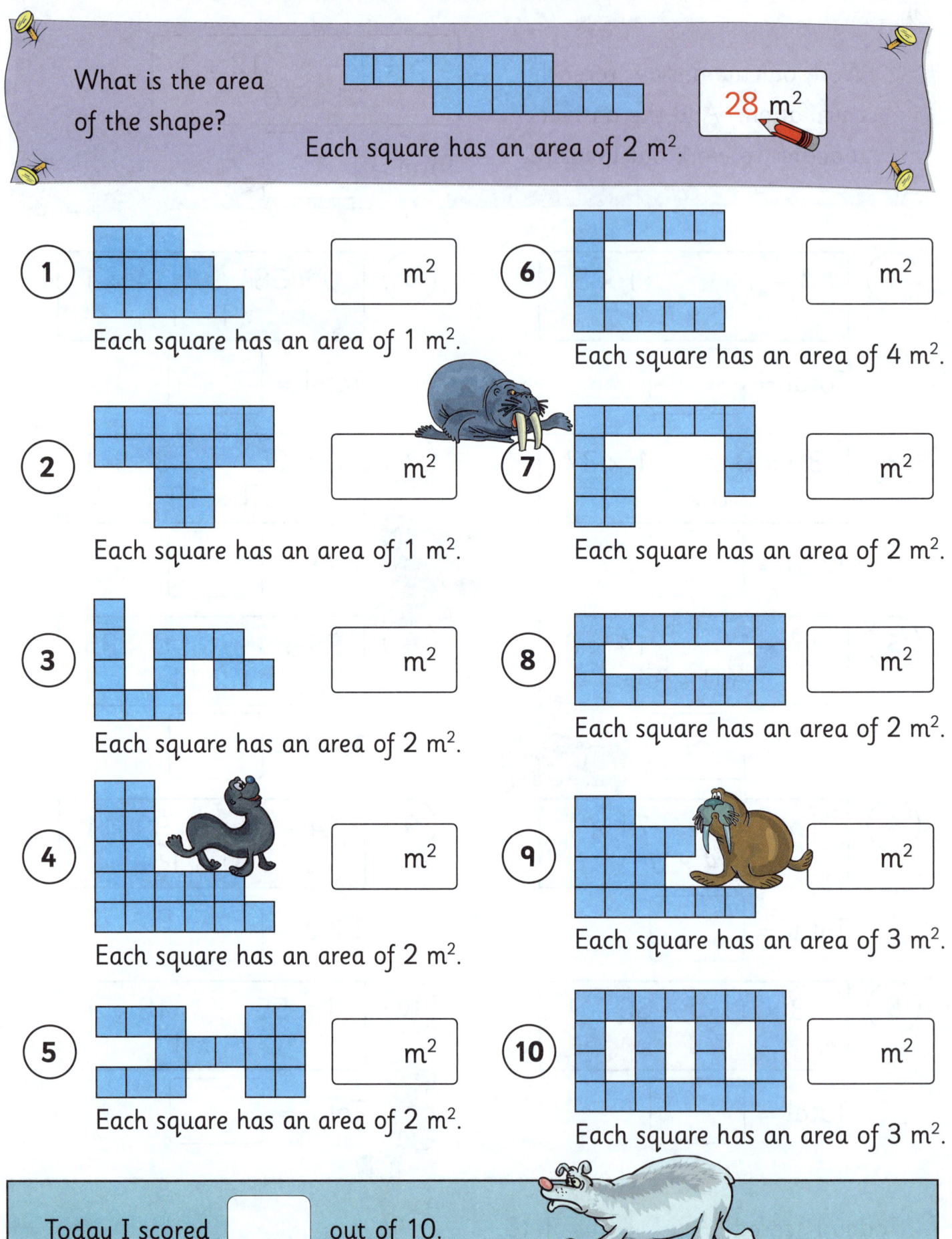

Week 7 — Day 3

Fill in the boxes to make the number sentence correct.

6 × 10 = 12 × **5** = **60**

1) 10 × 3 = 5 × ☐ = ☐

2) 4 × 6 = 8 × ☐ = ☐

3) 8 ÷ 2 = 16 ÷ ☐ = ☐

4) 20 ÷ 5 = 40 ÷ ☐ = ☐

5) 16 × 3 = 4 × ☐ = ☐

6) 6 × 6 = 2 × ☐ = ☐

7) 9 × 8 = 3 × ☐ = ☐

8) 8 × 7 = 2 × ☐ = ☐

9) 72 ÷ 12 = 36 ÷ ☐ = ☐

10) 42 ÷ 6 = 84 ÷ ☐ = ☐

11) 5 × 8 = 80 ÷ ☐ = ☐

12) 72 ÷ 2 = 9 × ☐ = ☐

Today I scored ☐ out of 12.

Week 7 — Day 4

Solve the calculation.   2 × 3 × 7 = 42

1) 10 × 5 × 2 =

2) 8 × 6 × 1 =

3) 2 × 0 × 10 =

4) 3 × 2 × 8 =

5) 4 × 5 × 2 =

6) 3 × 3 × 6 =

7) 5 × 2 × 5 =

8) 4 × 2 × 8 =

9) 3 × 7 × 3 =

10) 2 × 2 × 12 =

11) 5 × 10 × 10 =

12) 9 × 6 × 10 =

Today I scored [ ] out of 12.

Week 7 — Day 5

The table shows how Stuart spent his money. Work out the totals to complete the table. Fill in the box to complete the sentence.

	Lunch	Bus
Fri	£1.80	£2.50
Sat	£4.00	£1.50
Sun	£1.80	£2.50
Total	£7.60	£6.50

Stuart spent £1.10 more on lunch than on the bus.

1

	Train	Taxi
Fri	£6.00	£5.20
Sat	£0	£6.60
Sun	£6.00	£0
Total		

Stuart spent £ ____ more on the train than on taxis.

2

	Laundry	Cat food
Fri	£3.15	£1.20
Sat	£0	£1.20
Sun	£2.10	£1.20
Total		

Stuart spent £ ____ more on laundry than on cat food.

3

	Cinema	Breakfast
Fri	£11.25	£6.10
Sat	£0	£3.50
Sun	£8.75	£11.20
Total		

Stuart spent £ ____ more on breakfast than on the cinema.

4

	Tea	Snacks
Fri	£1.50	£2.40
Sat	£4.50	£3.80
Sun	£1.50	£2.40
Total		

Stuart spent £ ____ more on snacks than on tea.

Today I scored ____ out of 4.

Week 8 — Day 1

The table shows the number of pets owned by the pupils in a class. Who has the most pets?

	Dogs	Cats	Fish
Abed	0	0	7
Beth	0	3	0
Chris	2	1	5
Dora	1	1	3

Chris

1

	Dogs	Cats	Fish
Ellie	1	2	3
Felix	2	0	0
Gem	0	1	4
Hiro	2	1	0

4

	Dogs	Cats	Fish
Quinn	0	4	0
Rich	1	1	2
Sarah	2	2	1
Tom	0	1	3

2

	Dogs	Cats	Fish
Isla	0	1	0
Jack	1	2	4
Kate	0	3	3
Leo	1	0	1

5

	Dogs	Cats	Fish
Urma	0	0	7
Vince	0	3	0
Wini	2	1	5
Xavi	1	1	3

3

	Dogs	Cats	Fish
Mia	1	0	5
Nick	2	2	0
Olivia	2	1	2
Pete	3	1	1

6

	Dogs	Cats	Fish
Yvette	2	2	4
Zeb	1	3	4
Aria	3	2	3
Brian	1	4	4

Today I scored ☐ out of 6.

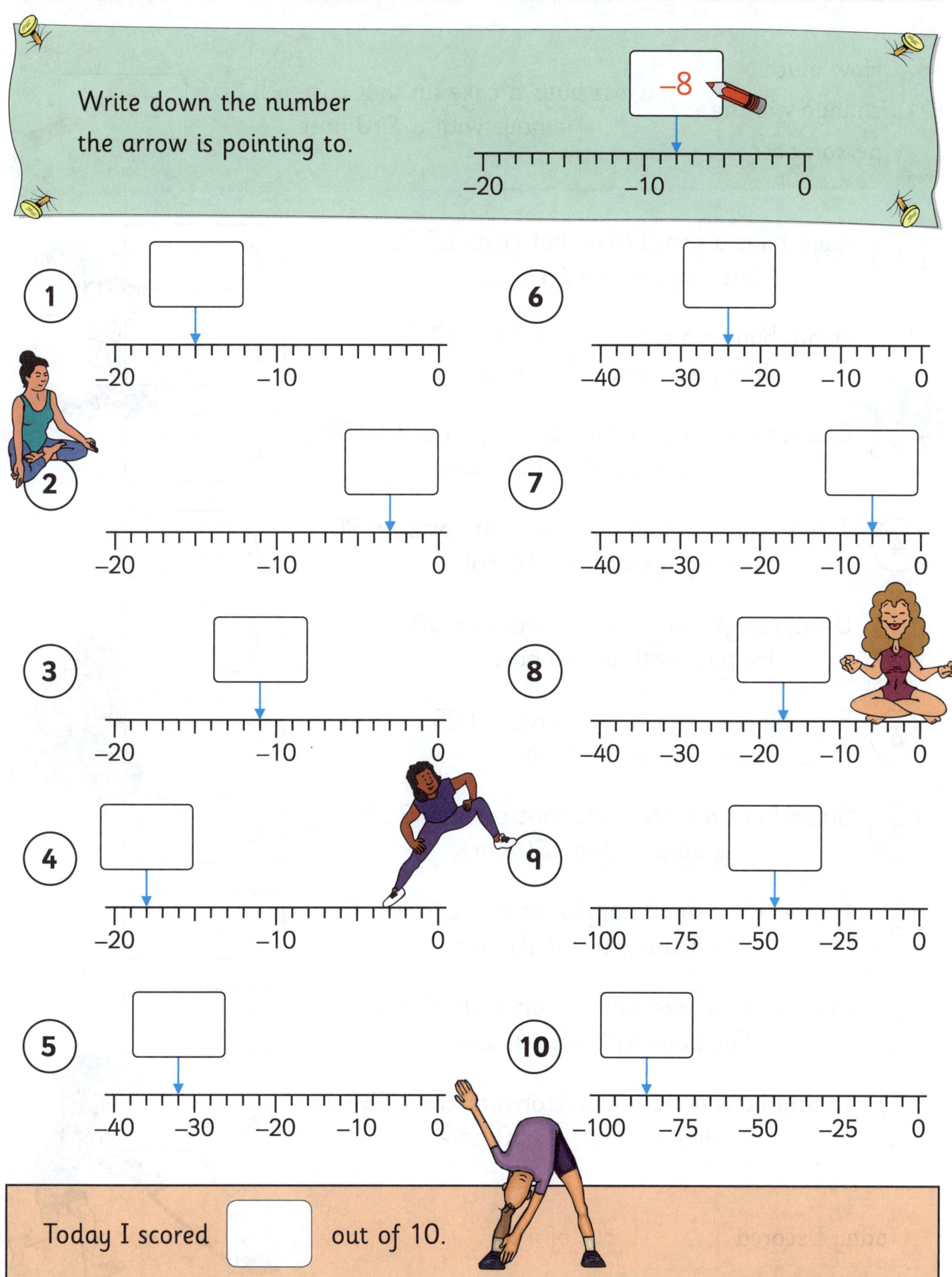

Week 8 — Day 3

How much change will the person get?

Lukasz buys a cake tin that costs £5.50. He pays with a £10 note.

£4.50

1. Kaya buys a pencil case that costs £2.70. She pays with a £5 note. £ ___

2. Nandi buys a hairbrush that costs £7.20. She pays with a £10 note. £ ___

3. Chelsea buys a baseball cap that costs £12.50. She pays with a £20 note. £ ___

4. Jarvis buys a colouring book that costs £6.90. He pays with a £10 note. £ ___

5. Usman buys a radio that costs £18.80. He pays with a £20 note. £ ___

6. Faye buys a toy cat that costs £3.85. She pays with a £5 note. £ ___

7. Steph buys a skateboard that costs £42.50. She pays with a £50 note. £ ___

8. Hunter buys some sunglasses that cost £8.25. He pays with a £10 note. £ ___

9. Elana buys a bike helmet that costs £16.35. She pays with a £20 note. £ ___

10. Chirag buys a metal detector that costs £34.75. He pays with a £50 note. £ ___

Today I scored ___ out of 10.

Week 8 — Day 4

Fill in the boxes in the calculation.

18 × 6 = [10 × 6] + 8 × 6 = [60] + [48] = [108]

1) 24 × 5 = 20 × 5 + [ ] × 5 = [ ] + [ ] = [ ]

2) 17 × 8 = 10 × 8 + [ ] × 8 = [ ] + [ ] = [ ]

3) 22 × 9 = [ ] × 9 + 2 × 9 = [ ] + [ ] = [ ]

4) 19 × 8 = [ ] × 8 + 9 × 8 = [ ] + [ ] = [ ]

5) 16 × 7 = [ ] × 7 + 6 × 7 = [ ] + [ ] = [ ]

6) 26 × 6 = 20 × 6 + [ ] × 6 = [ ] + [ ] = [ ]

7) 23 × 8 = 20 × 8 + [ ] × 8 = [ ] + [ ] = [ ]

8) 29 × 6 = [ ] × 6 + 9 × 6 = [ ] + [ ] = [ ]

9) 28 × 7 = 20 × 7 + [ ] × 7 = [ ] + [ ] = [ ]

10) 27 × 9 = [ ] × 9 + 7 × 9 = [ ] + [ ] = [ ]

Today I scored [ ] out of 10.

Week 8 — Day 5

What number did the person think of?

Sufjan thinks of a number. He divides it by 3, adds 24, then multiplies the answer by 2. He gets the number 60.

1 Kirsty thinks of a number. She multiplies it by 3, adds 4, then divides the answer by 5. She gets the number 8.

2 Phil thinks of a number. He divides it by 5, adds 18, then multiplies the answer by 2. He gets the number 42.

3 Ada thinks of a number. She multiplies it by 4, adds 16, then divides the answer by 4. She gets the number 12.

4 Charles thinks of a number. He multiplies it by 5, adds 9, then divides the answer by 11. He gets the number 4.

5 Jason thinks of a number. He divides it by 3, subtracts 4, then multiplies the answer by 8. He gets the number 56.

6 Owain thinks of a number. He divides it by 3, adds 5, then multiplies the answer by 2. He gets the number 28.

7 Rhonda thinks of a number. She divides it by 2, subtracts 3, then multiplies the answer by 9. She gets the number 54.

8 Phoebe thinks of a number. She multiplies it by 4, adds 4, then divides the answer by 12. She gets the number 7.

Today I scored ☐ out of 8.

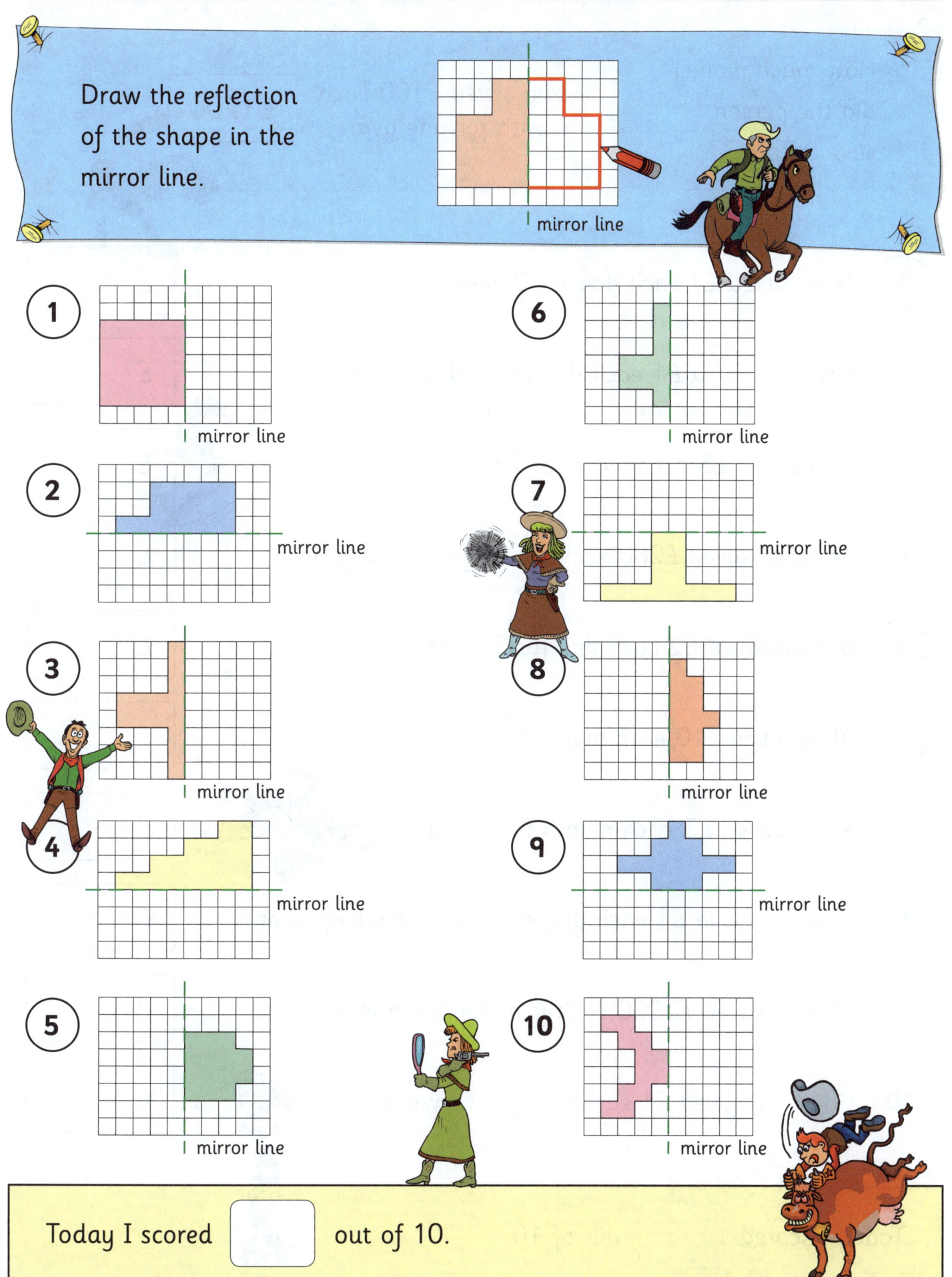

Week 9 — Day 2

How much money did the person save in total?

Adam saved £100 each month for one year. £1200

1) Jerry saved £1 each day for 2 weeks. £

2) Suzanne saved £1 each day every day in April. £

3) Ravi saved £5 each week for 28 days. £

4) Brandon saved £200 each month for half a year. £

5) Debbie saved £2 each day for 5 weeks. £

6) Alice saved £10 each month for 3 years. £

7) Aisha saved £5 each month for 5 years. £

8) Rowena saved £1 each day every day in a leap year. £

9) Marcus saved £1500 each year for 24 months. £

10) Courtney saved £1 each day for 12 weeks. £

Today I scored ☐ out of 10.

Week 9 — Day 3

Look at the grid. Write down the coordinates of each point.

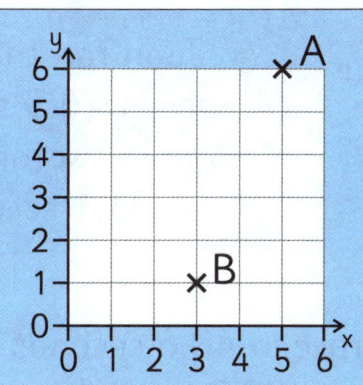

A = (5, 6)
B = (3, 1)

1
C =
D =

2
K =
L =

3
R =
S =

4
P =
Q =

5
F =
G =

6
Y =
Z =

Today I scored ⬜ out of 6.

Week 9 — Day 4

What was the total time taken for the runner to finish two races?

Juan ran the first race in 26.3 seconds and the second race in 31.1 seconds.

57.4 seconds

1. Martina ran the first race in 40.6 seconds and the second race in 38.3 seconds. _____ seconds

2. Craig ran the first race in 38.7 seconds and the second race in 30.1 seconds. _____ seconds

3. Prisha ran the first race in 36.0 seconds and the second race in 43.5 seconds. _____ seconds

4. Oliver ran the first race in 36.8 seconds and the second race in 32.9 seconds. _____ seconds

5. Vincent ran the first race in 23.9 seconds and the second race in 28.0 seconds. _____ seconds

6. Amrita ran the first race in 23.0 seconds and the second race in 27.6 seconds. _____ seconds

7. Will ran the first race in 30.8 seconds and the second race in 32.2 seconds. _____ seconds

8. Marvin ran the first race in 33.8 seconds and the second race in 25.9 seconds. _____ seconds

9. Lily ran the first race in 41.1 seconds and the second race in 39.9 seconds. _____ seconds

10. Samantha ran the first race in 27.6 seconds and the second race in 28.8 seconds. _____ seconds

Today I scored _____ out of 10.

Week 9 — Day 5

Draw the point on the grid. Join the point to complete the shape. Write down the name of the shape that is made.

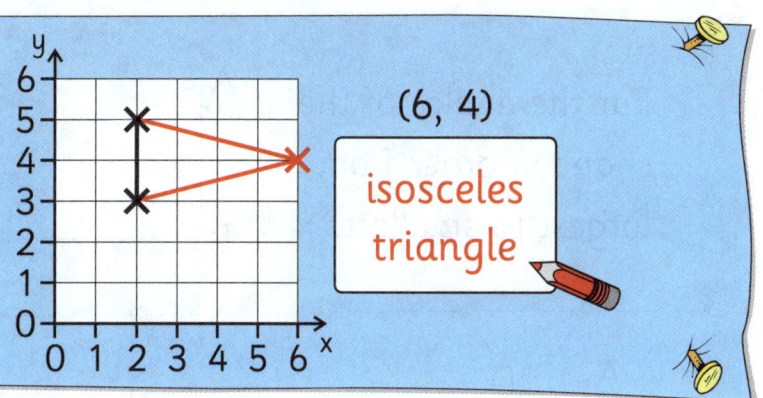

(6, 4) — isosceles triangle

1 (5, 5)

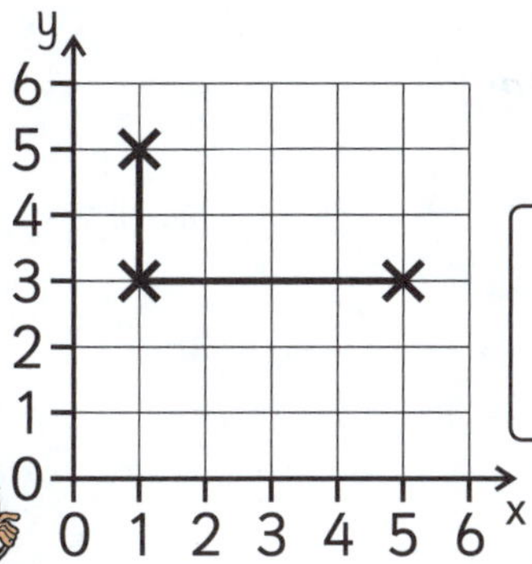

2 (3, 1)

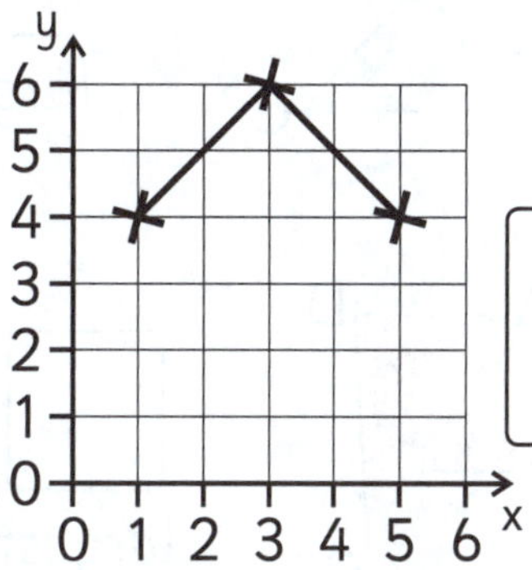

3 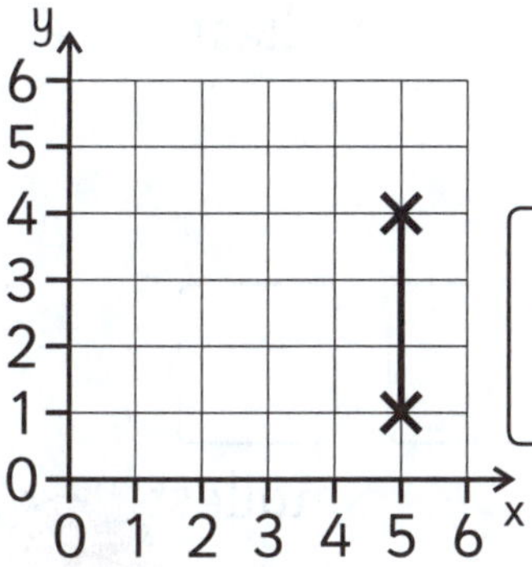 (0, 4)

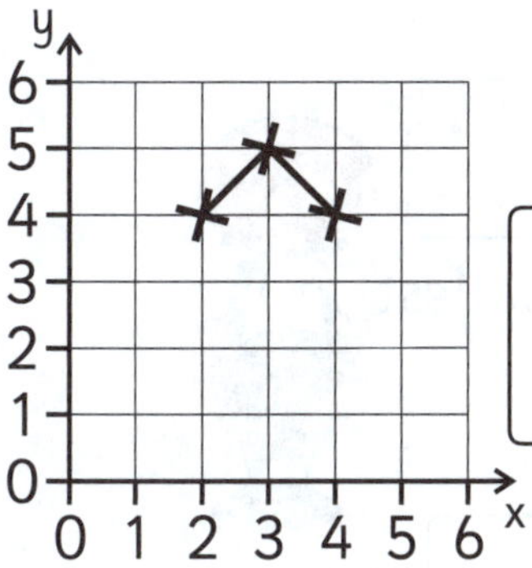

4 (3, 2)

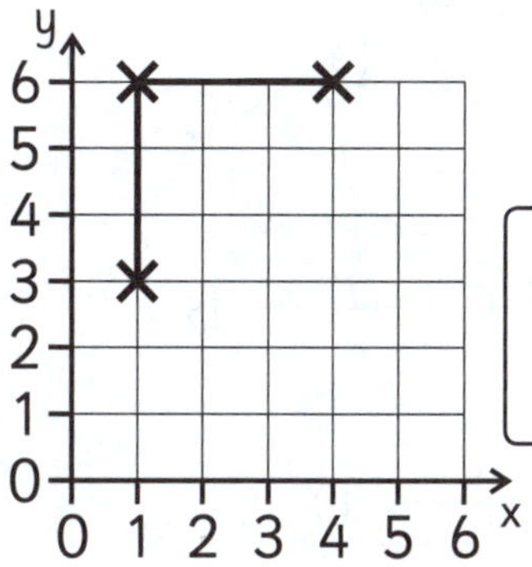

5 (4, 1)

6 (5, 0)

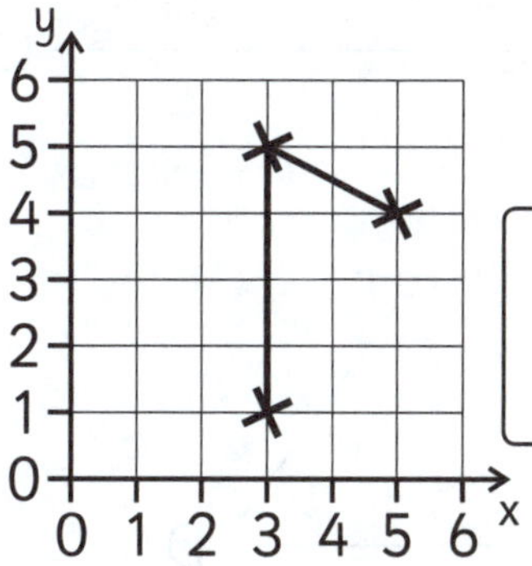

Today I scored ☐ out of 6.

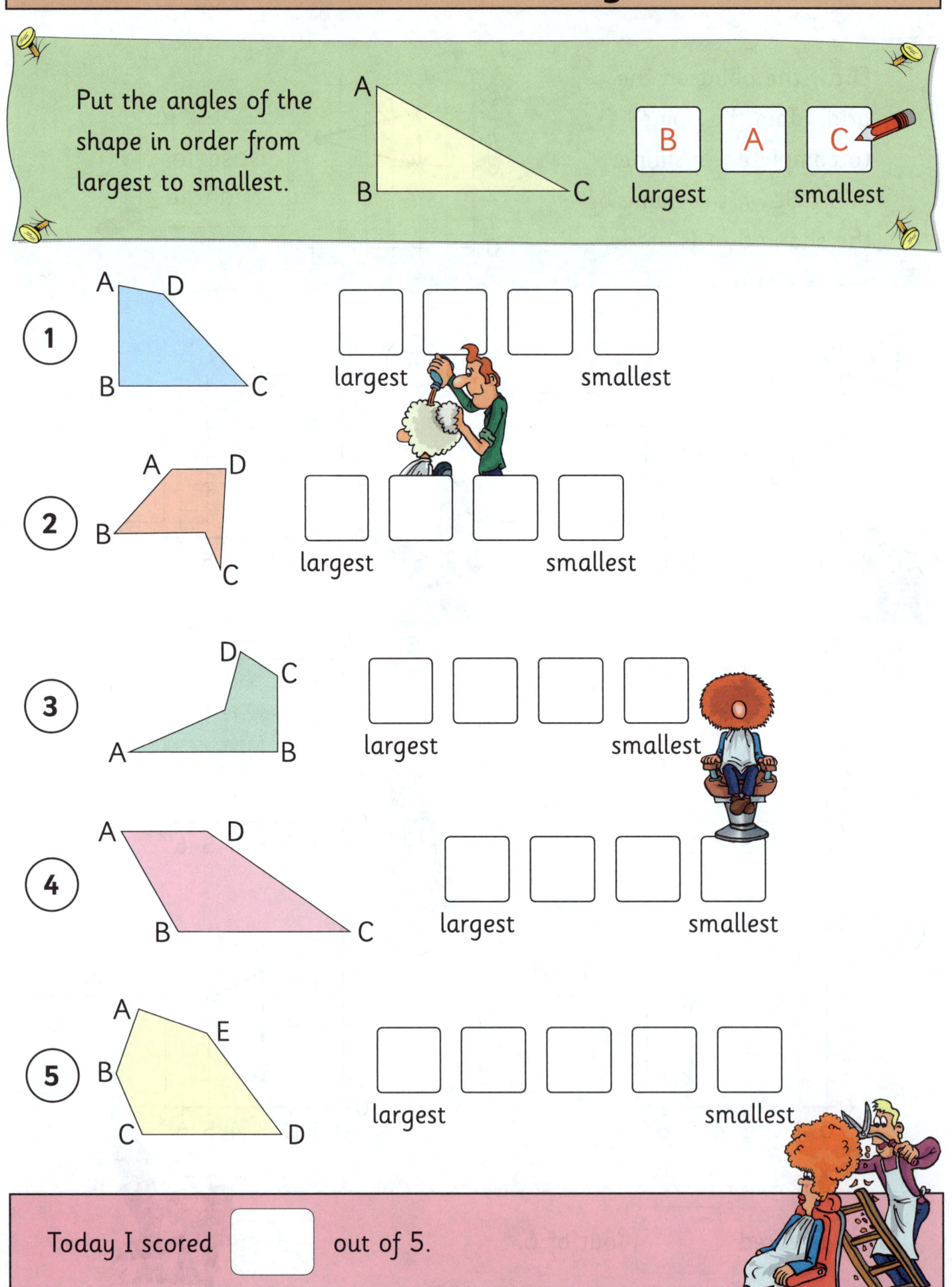

Week 10 — Day 2

Look at the shape and write a number in each box to describe its angles.

[pentagon shape] **3** obtuse angles
0 acute angles

1. [triangle] ☐ obtuse angles ☐ acute angles
2. [rhombus] ☐ obtuse angles ☐ acute angles
3. [trapezium] ☐ obtuse angles ☐ acute angles
4. [quadrilateral] ☐ obtuse angles ☐ acute angles
5. [triangle] ☐ obtuse angles ☐ acute angles
6. [parallelogram] ☐ obtuse angles ☐ acute angles
7. [pentagon] ☐ obtuse angles ☐ acute angles
8. [right triangle] ☐ obtuse angles ☐ acute angles
9. [quadrilateral] ☐ obtuse angles ☐ acute angles
10. [pentagon] ☐ obtuse angles ☐ acute angles

Today I scored ☐ out of 10.

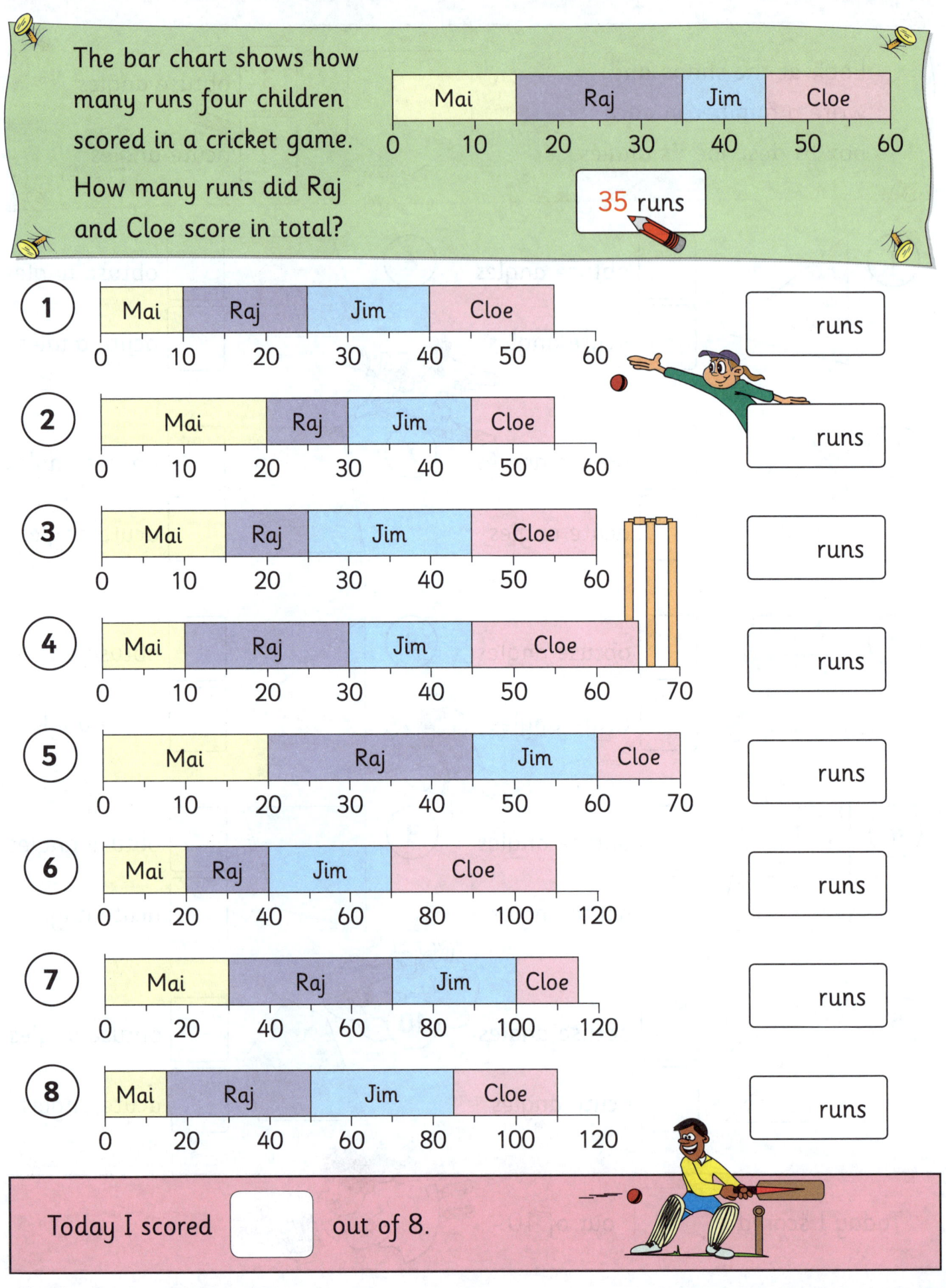

Week 10 — Day 4

Fill in the answer to the calculation.

4142 + 3809 = 7951

```
  4142
+ 3809
  ————
  7951
     1
```

1) 8757 − 7645 =

2) 6586 + 2304 =

3) 5934 + 3515 =

4) 9947 − 6751 =

5) 2682 + 3409 =

6) 9261 − 8937 =

7) 5691 + 3540 =

8) 4418 − 1935 =

9) 2877 + 4634 =

10) 7663 − 1788 =

Today I scored ☐ out of 10.

Week 10 — Day 5

Work out the number of pupils in the missing class.

Mrs Davies teaches four classes. She teaches 123 pupils in total. Two classes have 32 pupils each and one class has 28 pupils.

31 pupils

1) Mr Atkinson teaches five classes. He teaches 149 pupils in total. Three classes have 30 pupils each and one class has 28 pupils.

____ pupils

____ pupils

2) Miss Jakeman teaches six classes. She teaches 169 pupils in total. Two classes have 31 pupils each and three classes have 25 pupils each.

3) Mr Peck teaches seven classes. He teaches 175 pupils in total. Four classes have 25 pupils each and two classes have 26 pupils each.

____ pupils

____ pupils

4) Miss Bailey teaches eight classes. She teaches 208 pupils in total. Two classes have 28 pupils each and five classes have 25 pupils each.

5) Mr Chotai teaches nine classes. He teaches 191 pupils in total. Five classes have 22 pupils each and three classes have 19 pupils each.

____ pupils

Today I scored [ ] out of 5.

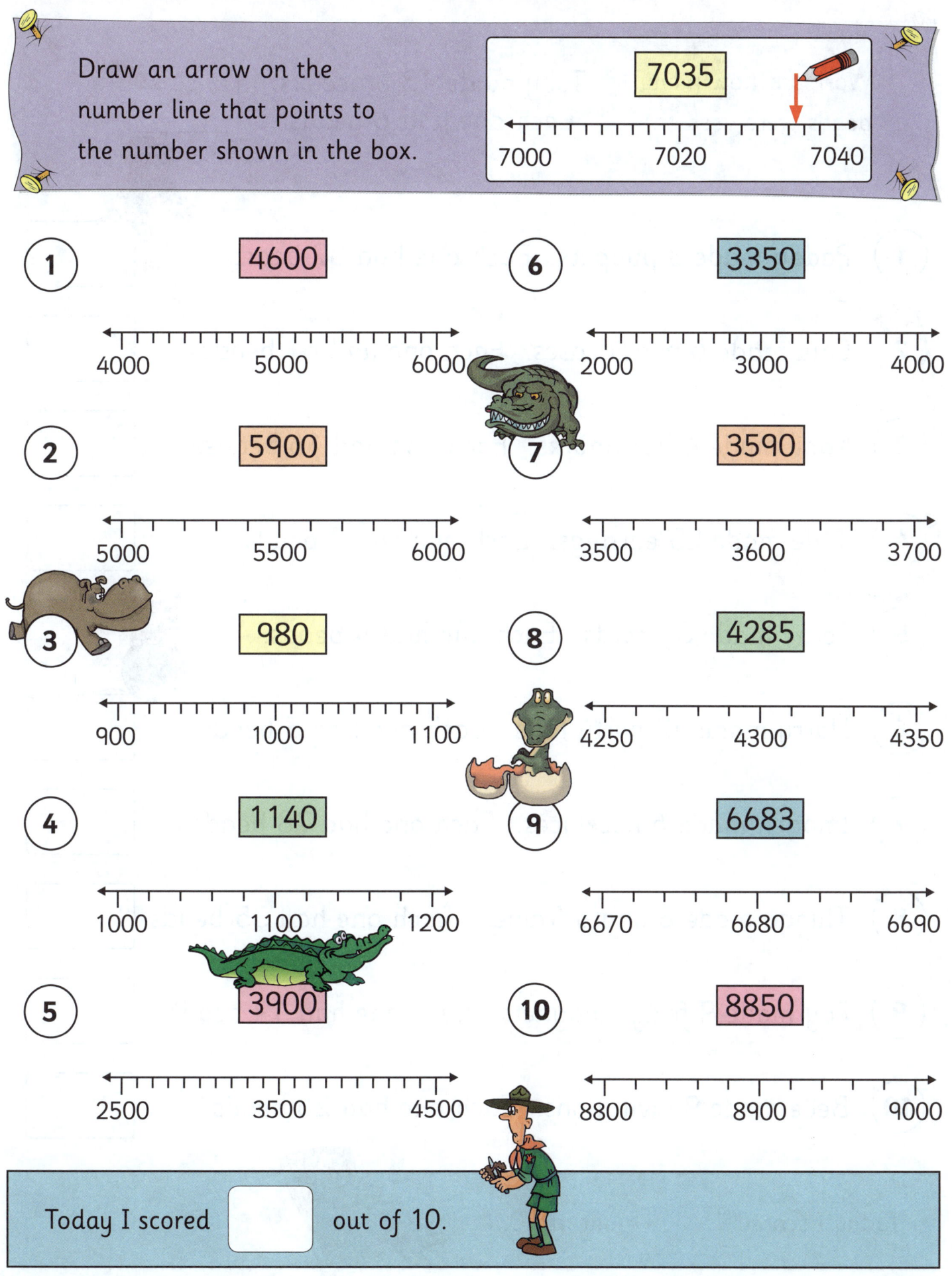

Week 11 — Day 2

Work out how many beads were used.

Toby made 13 bracelets. Each one had 6 beads. **78**

1) Paddy made 3 puppets. Each one had 32 beads.

2) Orla made 6 pencil cases. Each one had 61 beads.

3) Kapil made 4 bookmarks. Each one had 16 beads.

4) Jude made 25 earrings. Each one had 7 beads.

5) Ferne made 89 cards. Each one had 4 beads.

6) Harry made 42 party hats. Each one had 5 beads.

7) Imogen made 6 necklaces. Each one had 78 beads.

8) Thiago made 8 photo frames. Each one had 35 beads.

9) Fay made 9 fridge magnets. Each one had 19 beads.

10) Belle made 9 invitations. Each one had 26 beads.

Today I scored ☐ out of 10.

Week 11 — Day 3

Circle the fraction inside the box that is **not** equivalent to the fraction outside the box.

$\frac{1}{3}$ | $\frac{10}{30}$ $\frac{3}{9}$ (⃝$\frac{3}{6}$)

1) $\frac{1}{2}$ | $\frac{2}{5}$ $\frac{5}{10}$ $\frac{3}{6}$

2) $\frac{3}{4}$ | $\frac{8}{10}$ $\frac{6}{8}$ $\frac{15}{20}$

3) $\frac{2}{3}$ | $\frac{12}{18}$ $\frac{3}{4}$ $\frac{4}{6}$

4) $\frac{1}{4}$ | $\frac{2}{5}$ $\frac{2}{8}$ $\frac{5}{20}$

5) $\frac{2}{6}$ | $\frac{1}{3}$ $\frac{1}{2}$ $\frac{4}{12}$

6) $\frac{1}{5}$ | $\frac{2}{10}$ $\frac{4}{20}$ $\frac{5}{15}$

7) $\frac{3}{5}$ | $\frac{12}{20}$ $\frac{6}{10}$ $\frac{10}{15}$

8) $\frac{2}{4}$ | $\frac{6}{12}$ $\frac{4}{6}$ $\frac{8}{16}$

9) $\frac{2}{5}$ | $\frac{5}{12}$ $\frac{20}{50}$ $\frac{4}{10}$

10) $\frac{4}{5}$ | $\frac{12}{15}$ $\frac{7}{10}$ $\frac{16}{20}$

11) $\frac{5}{6}$ | $\frac{10}{12}$ $\frac{8}{9}$ $\frac{15}{18}$

12) $\frac{1}{6}$ | $\frac{4}{18}$ $\frac{10}{60}$ $\frac{2}{12}$

Today I scored ☐ out of 12.

Week 11 — Day 4

Work out the answer to the multiplication.

305 × 6 = 1830

$$\begin{array}{r} 305 \\ \times 6 \\ \hline 1830 \\ {\scriptstyle 3} \end{array}$$

1) 273 × 3 =

2) 405 × 4 =

3) 198 × 5 =

4) 849 × 3 =

5) 619 × 4 =

6) 128 × 6 =

7) 478 × 8 =

8) 572 × 7 =

9) 268 × 9 =

10) 496 × 7 =

Today I scored ☐ out of 10.

Week 11 — Day 5

How many baked goods were eaten? Eden baked 120 cupcakes and 90 brownies. $\frac{1}{5}$ of the cupcakes and $\frac{1}{3}$ of the brownies were eaten.

54

1. Suzy baked 64 lemon slices and 60 cookies. $\frac{1}{8}$ of the lemon slices and $\frac{1}{6}$ of the cookies were eaten.

2. Lilly baked 120 biscuits and 54 flapjacks. $\frac{1}{10}$ of the biscuits and $\frac{2}{9}$ of the flapjacks were eaten.

3. Sajid baked 36 French fancies and 18 treacle tarts. $\frac{1}{4}$ of the French fancies and $\frac{2}{3}$ of the treacle tarts were eaten.

4. Patrick baked 24 jam tarts and 49 apple pies. $\frac{2}{8}$ of the jam tarts and $\frac{5}{7}$ of the apple pies were eaten.

5. Geraint baked 81 scones and 300 gingerbread men. $\frac{8}{9}$ of the scones and $\frac{5}{6}$ of the gingerbread men were eaten.

6. Kian baked 160 muffins and 120 macaroons. $\frac{3}{4}$ of the muffins and $\frac{2}{5}$ of the macaroons were eaten.

Today I scored ☐ out of 6.

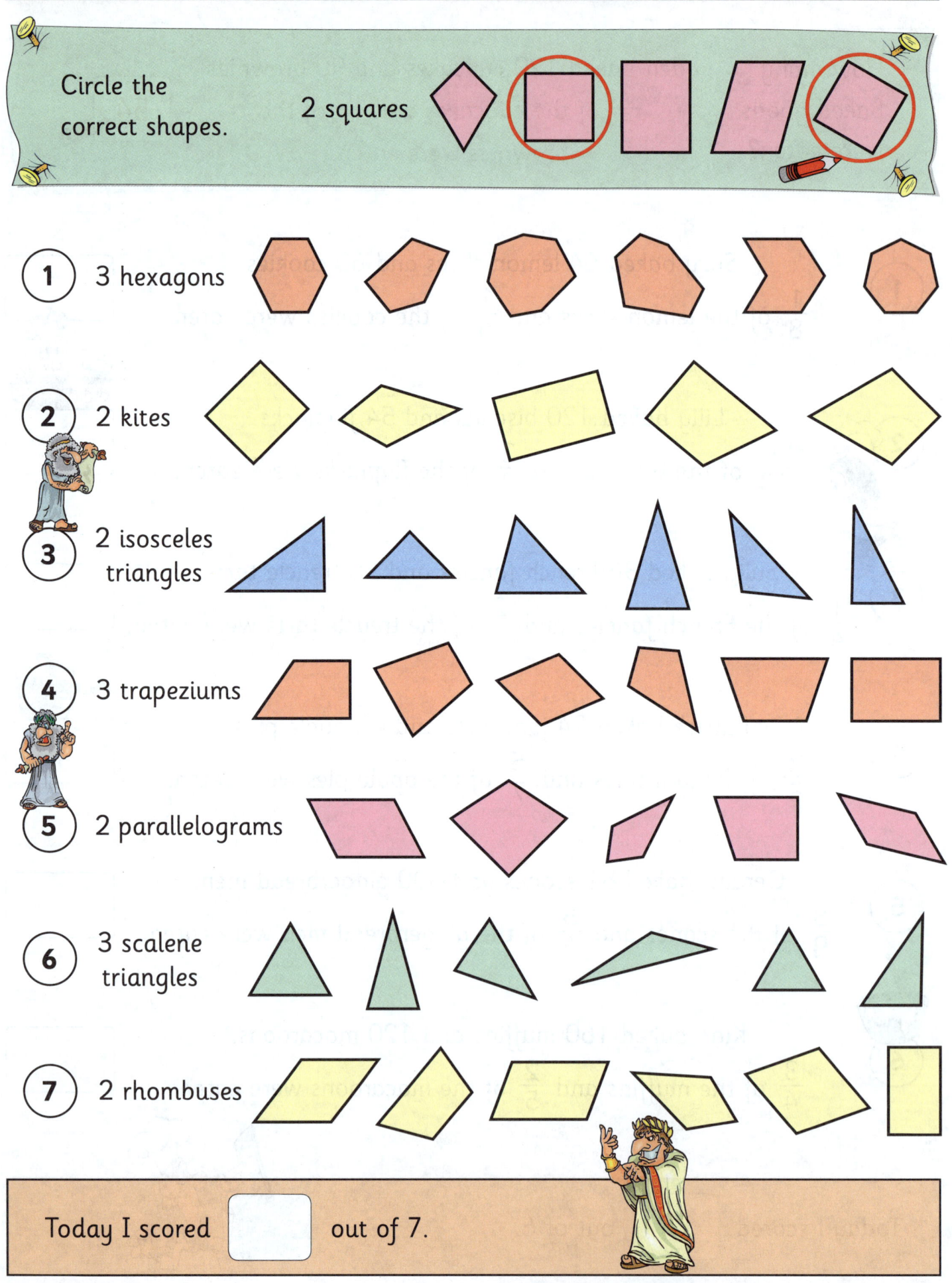

Week 12 — Day 2

Solve the calculation. $\frac{2}{8} + \frac{3}{8} = \frac{5}{8}$

1) $\frac{1}{6} + \frac{4}{6} =$ ☐

2) $\frac{3}{5} + \frac{4}{5} =$ ☐

3) $\frac{8}{11} - \frac{5}{11} =$ ☐

4) $\frac{13}{7} - \frac{4}{7} =$ ☐

5) $\frac{11}{10} + \frac{6}{10} =$ ☐

6) $\frac{12}{9} - \frac{4}{9} =$ ☐

7) $\frac{3}{6} + \frac{2}{6} + \frac{3}{6} =$ ☐

8) $\frac{2}{7} + \frac{3}{7} + \frac{8}{7} =$ ☐

9) $\frac{14}{12} - \frac{2}{12} - \frac{5}{12} =$ ☐

10) $\frac{17}{10} - \frac{6}{10} - \frac{10}{10} =$ ☐

11) $\frac{23}{50} + \frac{14}{50} + \frac{27}{50} =$ ☐

12) $\frac{61}{40} - \frac{27}{40} - \frac{16}{40} =$ ☐

Today I scored ☐ out of 12.

Week 12 — Day 3

How far was Penny's journey?

A bus travelled 20 km. Penny rode on the bus for $\frac{2}{5}$ of its journey.

8 km

1) A bus travelled 70 km. Penny rode on the bus for $\frac{1}{2}$ of its journey. ☐ km

2) A bus travelled 100 km. Penny rode on the bus for $\frac{1}{5}$ of its journey. ☐ km

3) A bus travelled 48 km. Penny rode on the bus for $\frac{1}{4}$ of its journey. ☐ km

4) A bus travelled 800 m. Penny rode on the bus for $\frac{3}{4}$ of its journey. ☐ m

5) A bus travelled 27 km. Penny rode on the bus for $\frac{2}{3}$ of its journey. ☐ km

6) A bus travelled 90 km. Penny rode on the bus for $\frac{3}{10}$ of its journey. ☐ km

7) A bus travelled 2500 m. Penny rode on the bus for $\frac{4}{5}$ of its journey. ☐ m

8) A bus travelled 6000 m. Penny rode on the bus for $\frac{7}{10}$ of its journey. ☐ m

Today I scored ☐ out of 8.

Week 12 — Day 4

Joe buys some identical pieces of turf to cover his garden. Use the diagram to work out the perimeter of the garden.

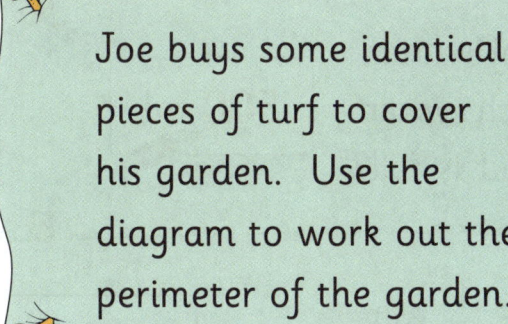 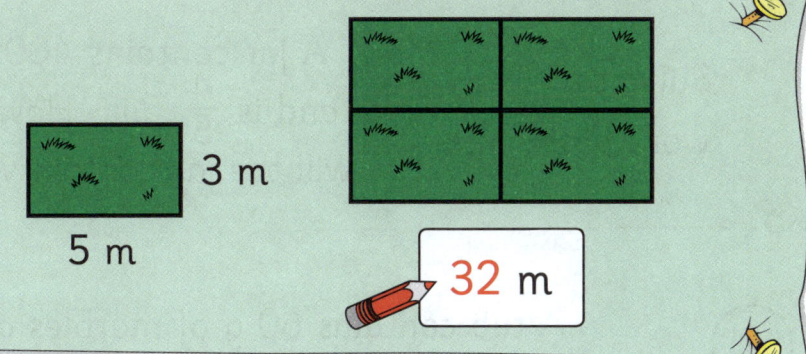

32 m

1. 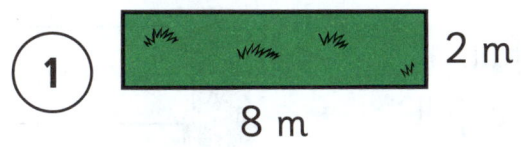  ☐ m

2.    ☐ m

3. 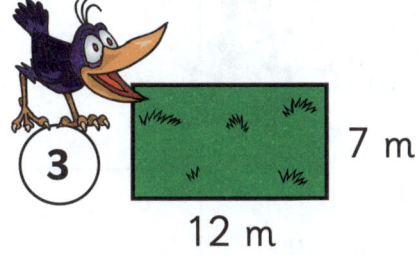  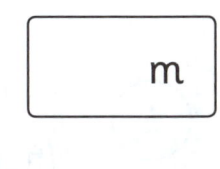 ☐ m

4. 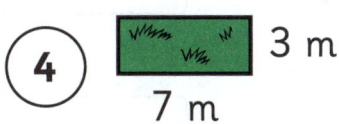  ☐ m

Today I scored ☐ out of 4.

Week 12 — Day 5

Solve the word problem.

A jar contains 400 ml of water and is $\frac{4}{5}$ full. How much water will the jar contain when it is full?

500 ml

1) A tub contains 60 g of marbles and is $\frac{1}{2}$ full. What weight of marbles will the tub contain when it is full? ☐ g

2) A jug contains 20 ml of milk and is $\frac{1}{5}$ full. How much milk will the jug contain when it is full? ☐ ml

3) A mug contains 80 ml of tea and is $\frac{1}{3}$ full. How much tea will the mug contain when it is full? ☐ ml

4) A box contains 125 g of building blocks and is $\frac{1}{4}$ full. What weight of blocks will the box contain when it is full? ☐ g

5) A bottle contains 400 ml of water and is $\frac{2}{3}$ full. How much water will the bottle contain when it is full? ☐ ml

6) A tin contains 80 g of biscuits and is $\frac{2}{5}$ full. What weight of biscuits will the tin contain when it is full? ☐ g

7) A jar contains 240 g of jam and is $\frac{4}{5}$ full. What weight of jam will the jar contain when it is full? ☐ g

8) A carton contains 150 ml of juice and is $\frac{3}{8}$ full. How much juice will the carton contain when it is full? ☐ ml

Today I scored ☐ out of 8.

Answers

Week 1 — Day 1
1. 0.64, 1.25, 1.43, 1.86
2. 0.21, 1.18, 1.60, 1.80
3. 0.67, 1.06, 1.49, 1.79
4. 1.26, 1.35, 1.84, 1.92
5. 1.08, 1.29, 1.47, 1.74
6. 1.10, 1.14, 1.38, 1.89
7. 1.72, 1.76, 1.82, 1.94
8. 1.32, 1.45, 1.54, 1.56

Week 1 — Day 2
1. 5644, 7644
2. 6368, 8368
3. 6422, 7422
4. 2536, 3536
5. 1179, 3179
6. 7887, 8887
7. 1953, 2953
8. 7795, 9795
9. 2342, 3342
10. 5925, 6925
11. 5688, 6688
12. 3876, 4876

Week 1 — Day 3
1. 2
2. 7
3. 6
4. 6
5. 8
6. 5
7. 5
8. 9
9. 4
10. 1
11. 9
12. 6

Week 1 — Day 4
1. 10
2. 0.5
3. 10
4. 10
5. 100
6. 100
7. 0.43
8. 8.6
9. 100
10. 0.9
11. 10
12. 0.06

Week 1 — Day 5
1. Annika
2. Forrest
3. Iwan
4. Tyra
5. Tahir
6. Mack
7. Aidan
8. Em

Week 2 — Day 1
1. 0.3
2. 0.9
3. 0.64
4. 0.17
5. 0.7
6. 0.32
7. 0.5
8. 0.99
9. 0.75
10. 0.05
11. 0.5
12. 0.02

Week 2 — Day 2
1. 32 cm
2. 12 cm
3. 27 cm
4. 24 cm
5. 16 cm
6. 48 cm
7. 35 cm
8. 560 cm
9. 240 cm
10. 92 cm

Week 2 — Day 3
1. 11:55
2. 01:45
3. 19:46
4. 03:00
5. 16:30
6. 17:15
7. 18:54
8. 22:30
9. 23:05
10. 08:37
11. 21:18
12. 00:44

Week 2 — Day 4
1. 1.5
2. 6.25
3. 35.5
4. 15.25
5. 79.4
6. 2.3
7. 52.75
8. 5.16
9. 21.7
10. 18.12

Week 2 — Day 5
1. 270 g
2. 230 g
3. 400 g
4. 300 g
5. 60 g
6. 133 g

Week 3 — Day 1
1. 1 right angle
2. 2 right angles
3. 3 right angles
4. 1 right angle
5. 2 right angles
6. 3 right angles
7. 3 right angles
8. 3 right angles
9. 2 right angles
10. 1 right angle

Week 3 — Day 2
1. 4000
2. 8500
3. 3000
4. 9000
5. 7500
6. 7500
7. 3500
8. 5500
9. 3500
10. 3500

Week 3 — Day 3
1. 68 minutes
2. 51 minutes
3. 46 minutes
4. 72 minutes
5. 81 minutes
6. 100 minutes
7. 126 minutes
8. 104 minutes
9. 187 minutes
10. 167 minutes

Week 3 — Day 4
1. 4000 m
2. 5 litres
3. 800 cm
4. 3200 g
5. 2.9 litres
6. 560 cm
7. 800 g
8. 1500 m
9. 0.65 litres
10. 1070 cm
11. 15 800 g
12. 930 m

Week 3 — Day 5
1. 1 h 40 min
2. 1 h 25 min
3. 2 h 10 min
4. 2 h 5 min
5. 2 h 50 min

Week 4 — Day 1
1. 5335
2. 7289
3. 10 494
4. 9682
5. 6165
6. 9715
7. 9341
8. 6222
9. 8123
10. 9051

Week 4 — Day 2
1. 32
2. 42
3. 22
4. 38
5. 26
6. 36

Week 4 — Day 3
1. 20 cm
2. 400 g
3. 5 cm
4. 2 m
5. 6 g
6. 70 cm
7. 8 m
8. 7 m
9. 1 kg
10. 60 g
11. 120 m
12. 14 kg

Week 4 — Day 4
1. Five 1 kg bags of sugar
2. Two 1 kg bags of flour
3. Three 80 g bags of chocolate chips
4. Four 300 g packs of butter
5. Two boxes of 15 eggs
6. Three 500 g jars of jam

Week 4 — Day 5
1.
Red	◇◇◇◇
Orange	◇◇◇
Yellow	◇

2.
Orange	◇
Yellow	◇◇
Green	◇◇◇

3.

Pink	◇◇◇◇
Orange	◇◇◇◇◇
Red	◇◇◇

4.

Purple	◇◇◁
Green	◇◇◇◁
Blue	◇◇

5.

Yellow	◇◇◇◇◁
Pink	◇◇◇◁
Red	◇◇◇◇

6.

Orange	◇◇
Blue	◁
Purple	◇◇◇◁

7.

Blue	◇◇◇◁
Purple	◇◇◇◇
Pink	◇◇◇◇◁

8.

Green	◇◁
Purple	◇◇◇
Yellow	◇◇◇◁

Week 5 — Day 1

1. 7
2. 14
3. 70
4. 35
5. 21
6. 28
7. 77
8. 42
9. 49
10. 63
11. 56
12. 84

Week 5 — Day 2

1. 1046
2. 3251
3. 1191
4. 2735
5. 1294
6. 2780
7. 1339
8. 3302
9. 2629
10. 3548

Week 5 — Day 3

1. 36, 45, **54**, **63**, **72**
2. 72, 81, **90**, **99**, **108**
3. 63, 54, **45**, **36**, **27**
4. **54**, 63, **72**, 81, **90**
5. **99**, **90**, 81, **72**, 63
6. **81**, 72, **63**, 54, **45**
7. 117, **108**, **99**, 90, **81**
8. **90**, 99, **108**, **117**, 126

Week 5 — Day 4

1. 05:08
2. 03:24
3. 20:03
4. 08:16
5. 15:12
6. 08:50
7. 16:20
8. 02:55
9. 16:38
10. 13:06

Week 5 — Day 5

1. **900** + 84 = **984**
2. **950** + 37 = **987**
3. **910** + 49 = **959**
4. **831** + 15 = **846**
5. **942** + 36 = **978**
6. **622** + 59 = **681**
7. **762** + 29 = **791**
8. **752** + 85 = **837**
9. **872** + 52 = **924**
10. **754** + 97 = **851**

Week 6 — Day 1

1.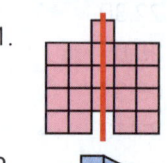
2.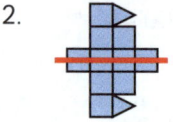
3.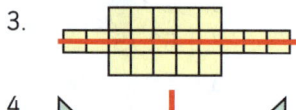
4.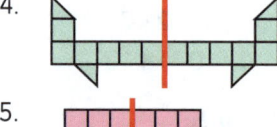
5.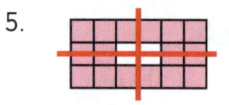
6.
7.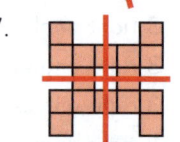
8.
9.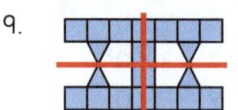
10.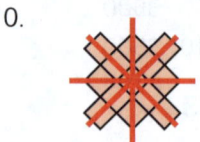

Week 6 — Day 2

1. 2390 − 1240 or 2390 − 1150
2. 4425 − 1725 or 4425 − 2700
3. 6760 + 1140, 1140 + 6760 or 7900 − 6760
4. 7815 − 6560 or 7815 − 1255
5. 3524 + 1575, 1575 + 3524 or 5099 − 3524
6. 76 − 48.5 or 76 − 27.5
7. 91.2 − 50.1 or 91.2 − 41.1
8. 6301 − 3812 or 6301 − 2489
9. 5.1 + 1.3, 1.3 + 5.1 or 6.4 − 5.1
10. 1219 + 1325, 1325 + 1219 or 2544 − 1219
11. 7276 − 5707 or 7276 − 1569
12. 2314 + 2054, 2054 + 2314 or 4368 − 2314

Week 6 — Day 3

1.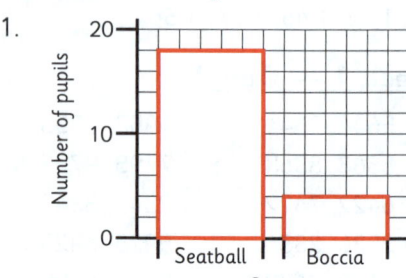
2.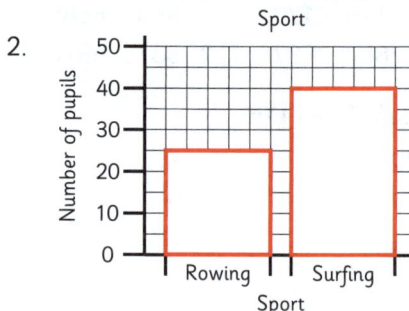
3.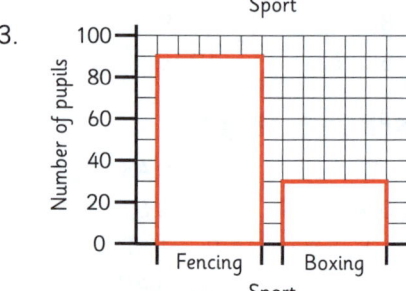
4.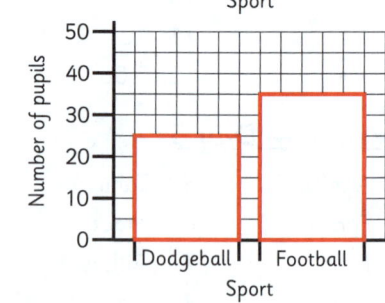

Week 6 — Day 4

1. £40
2. £35
3. £82
4. £81
5. £36
6. £66
7. £54
8. £91

Week 6 — Day 5

1. 16
2. 11
3. 22
4. 30

Answers

Week 7 — Day 1
1. 12
2. 43
3. 77
4. 85
5. 50
6. 93
7. 80
8. 104
9. 183
10. 102

Week 7 — Day 2
1. 12 m²
2. 16 m²
3. 24 m²
4. 34 m²
5. 30 m²
6. 48 m²
7. 26 m²
8. 32 m²
9. 45 m²
10. 66 m²

Week 7 — Day 3
1. 10 × 3 = 5 × **6** = **30**
2. 4 × 6 = 8 × **3** = **24**
3. 8 ÷ 2 = 16 ÷ **4** = **4**
4. 20 ÷ 5 = 40 ÷ **10** = **4**
5. 16 × 3 = 4 × **12** = **48**
6. 6 × 6 = 2 × **18** = **36**
7. 9 × 8 = 3 × **24** = **72**
8. 8 × 7 = 2 × **28** = **56**
9. 72 ÷ 12 = 36 ÷ **6** = **6**
10. 42 ÷ 6 = 84 ÷ **12** = **7**
11. 5 × 8 = 80 ÷ **2** = **40**
12. 72 ÷ 2 = 9 × **4** = **36**

Week 7 — Day 4
1. 100
2. 48
3. 0
4. 48
5. 40
6. 54
7. 50
8. 64
9. 63
10. 48
11. 500
12. 540

Week 7 — Day 5
1.

	Train	Taxi
Fri	£6.00	£5.20
Sat	£0	£6.60
Sun	£6.00	£0
Total	**£12.00**	**£11.80**

Stuart spent **£0.20** more on the train than on taxis.

2.

	Laundry	Cat food
Fri	£3.15	£1.20
Sat	£0	£1.20
Sun	£2.10	£1.20
Total	**£5.25**	**£3.60**

Stuart spent **£1.65** more on laundry than on cat food.

3.

	Cinema	Breakfast
Fri	£11.25	£6.10
Sat	£0	£3.50
Sun	£8.75	£11.20
Total	**£20.00**	**£20.80**

Stuart spent **£0.80** more on breakfast than on the cinema.

4.

	Tea	Snacks
Fri	£1.50	£2.40
Sat	£4.50	£3.80
Sun	£1.50	£2.40
Total	**£7.50**	**£8.60**

Stuart spent **£1.10** more on snacks than on tea.

Week 8 — Day 1
1. Ellie
2. Jack
3. Mia
4. Sarah
5. Wini
6. Brian

Week 8 — Day 2
1. −15
2. −3
3. −11
4. −18
5. −32
6. −24
7. −6
8. −17
9. −45
10. −85

Week 8 — Day 3
1. £2.30
2. £2.80
3. £7.50
4. £3.10
5. £1.20
6. £1.15
7. £7.50
8. £1.75
9. £3.65
10. £15.25

Week 8 — Day 4
1. 20 × 5 + **4** × 5 = **100** + **20** = **120**
2. 10 × 8 + **7** × 8 = **80** + **56** = **136**
3. **20** × 9 + 2 × 9 = **180** + **18** = **198**
4. **10** × 8 + 9 × 8 = **80** + **72** = **152**
5. **10** × 7 + 6 × 7 = **70** + **42** = **112**
6. 20 × 6 + **6** × 6 = **120** + **36** = **156**
7. 20 × 8 + **3** × 8 = **160** + **24** = **184**
8. **20** × 6 + 9 × 6 = **120** + **54** = **174**
9. 20 × 7 + **8** × 7 = **140** + **56** = **196**
10. **20** × 9 + 7 × 9 = **180** + **63** = **243**

Week 8 — Day 5
1. 12
2. 15
3. 8
4. 7
5. 33
6. 27
7. 18
8. 20

Week 9 — Day 1
1.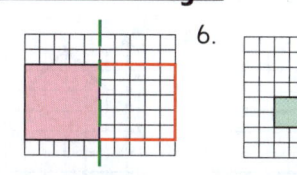
2.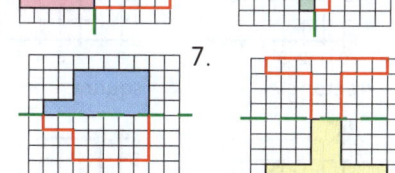
3.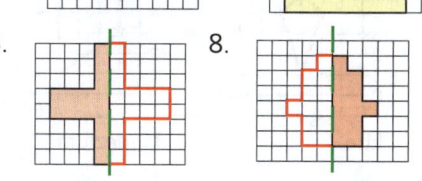
4.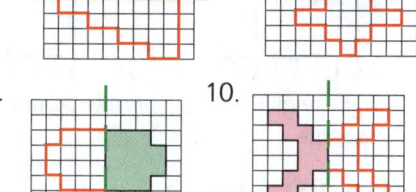
5.
6.
7.
8.
9.
10.

Week 9 — Day 2
1. £14
2. £30
3. £20
4. £1200
5. £70
6. £360
7. £300
8. £366
9. £3000
10. £84

Week 9 — Day 3
1. C = (4, 1)
   D = (4, 6)
2. K = (2, 4)
   L = (5, 2)
3. R = (4, 5)
   S = (2, 2)
4. P = (1, 3)
   Q = (3, 4)
5. F = (6, 5)
   G = (0, 2)
6. Y = (3, 0)
   Z = (5, 5)

Week 9 — Day 4
1. 78.9 seconds
2. 68.8 seconds
3. 79.5 seconds
4. 69.7 seconds
5. 51.9 seconds
6. 50.6 seconds
7. 63.0 seconds
8. 59.7 seconds
9. 81.0 seconds
10. 56.4 seconds

Week 9 — Day 5

1. 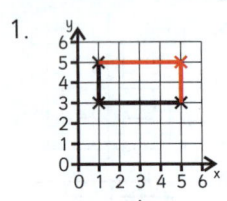 rectangle
4. 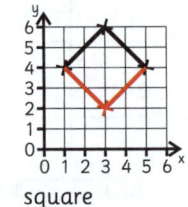 square
2. 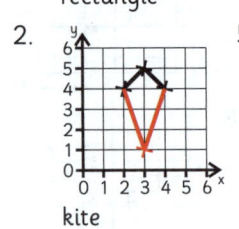 kite
5. 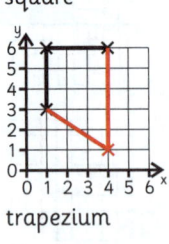 trapezium
3. 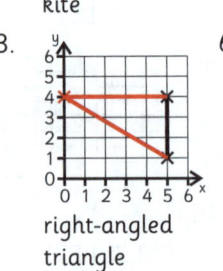 right-angled triangle
6. 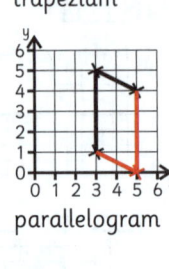 parallelogram

Week 10 — Day 1

1. D, B, A, C
2. A, D, B, C
3. C, B, D, A
4. D, B, A, C
5. E, B, C, A, D

Week 10 — Day 2

1. **0** obtuse angles, **3** acute angles
2. **2** obtuse angles, **2** acute angles
3. **2** obtuse angles, **2** acute angles
4. **1** obtuse angle, **1** acute angle
5. **1** obtuse angle, **2** acute angles
6. **2** obtuse angles, **2** acute angles
7. **4** obtuse angles, **1** acute angle
8. **1** obtuse angle, **2** acute angles
9. **1** obtuse angle, **2** acute angles
10. **4** obtuse angles, **1** acute angle

Week 10 — Day 3

1. 30 runs
2. 20 runs
3. 25 runs
4. 40 runs
5. 35 runs
6. 60 runs
7. 55 runs
8. 60 runs

Week 10 — Day 4

1. 1112
2. 8890
3. 9449
4. 3196
5. 6091
6. 324
7. 9231
8. 2483
9. 7511
10. 5875

Week 10 — Day 5

1. 31 pupils
2. 32 pupils
3. 23 pupils
4. 27 pupils
5. 24 pupils

Week 11 — Day 1

1.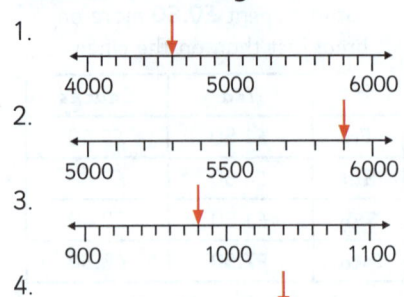
2.
3.
4.
5.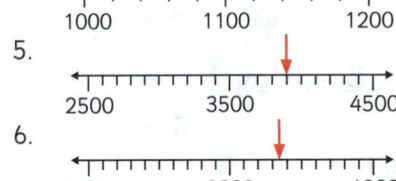
6.
7.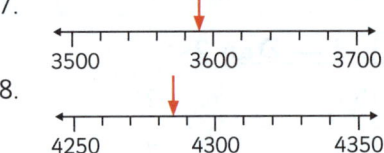
8.
9.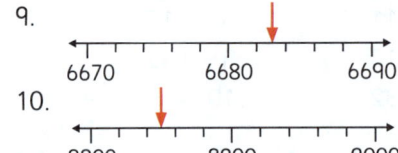
10.

Week 11 — Day 2

1. 96
2. 366
3. 64
4. 175
5. 356
6. 210
7. 468
8. 280
9. 171
10. 234

Week 11 — Day 3

1. $\frac{2}{5}$
2. $\frac{8}{10}$
3. $\frac{3}{4}$
4. $\frac{2}{5}$
5. $\frac{1}{2}$
6. $\frac{5}{15}$
7. $\frac{10}{15}$
8. $\frac{4}{6}$
9. $\frac{5}{12}$
10. $\frac{7}{10}$
11. $\frac{8}{9}$
12. $\frac{4}{18}$

Week 11 — Day 4

1. 819
2. 1620
3. 990
4. 2547
5. 2476
6. 768
7. 3824
8. 4004
9. 2412
10. 3472

Week 11 — Day 5

1. 18
2. 24
3. 21
4. 41
5. 322
6. 168

Week 12 — Day 1

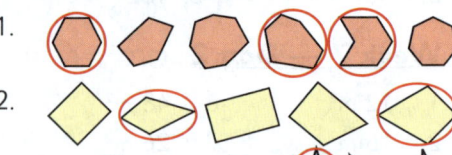
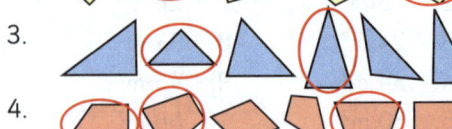

Week 12 — Day 2

1. $\frac{5}{6}$
2. $\frac{7}{5}$
3. $\frac{3}{11}$
4. $\frac{9}{7}$
5. $\frac{17}{10}$
6. $\frac{8}{9}$
7. $\frac{8}{6}$
8. $\frac{13}{7}$
9. $\frac{7}{12}$
10. $\frac{1}{10}$
11. $\frac{64}{50}$
12. $\frac{18}{40}$

Week 12 — Day 3

1. 35 km
2. 20 km
3. 12 km
4. 600 m
5. 18 km
6. 27 km
7. 2000 m
8. 4200 m

Week 12 — Day 4

1. 40 m
2. 72 m
3. 100 m
4. 80 m

Week 12 — Day 5

1. 120 g
2. 100 ml
3. 240 ml
4. 500 g
5. 600 ml
6. 200 g
7. 300 g
8. 400 ml